REACHING OUT TO LATINO FAMILIES OF ENGLISH LANGUAGE LEARNERS

ASCD
Alexandria, Virginia USA

Respete a los demás.

Esté preparado para aprender.

REACHING OUT TO LATINO FAMILIES OF ENGLISH LANGUAGE LEARNERS

David Campos • Rocio Delgado • Mary Esther Soto Huerta

ASCD®
1703 N. Beauregard St. • Alexandria, VA 22311-1714 USA
Phone: 800-933-2723 or 703-578-9600 • Fax: 703-575-5400
Website: www.ascd.org • E-mail: member@ascd.org
Author guidelines: www.ascd.org/write

Gene R. Carter, *Executive Director;* Judy Zimny, *Chief Program Development Officer;* Nancy Modrak, *Publisher;* Scott Willis, *Director, Book Acquisitions & Development;* Julie Houtz, *Director, Book Editing & Production;* Ernesto Yermoli, *Editor;* Greer Wymond, *Senior Graphic Designer;* Mike Kalyan, *Production Manager;* Valerie Younkin, *Desktop Publishing Specialist;* Sarah Plumb, *Production Specialist*

PAPERBACK ISBN: 978-1-4166-1272-8   ASCD product # 110005   n7/11

Also available as an e-book (see Books in Print for the ISBNs).

Quantity discounts for the paperback edition only: 10–49 copies, 10%; 50+ copies, 15%; for 1,000 or more copies, call 800-933-2723, ext. 5634, or 703-575-5634. For desk copies: member@ascd.org.

Library of Congress Cataloging-in-Publication Data
Campos, David.
Reaching out to Latino families of English language learners / David Campos, Rocio Delgado, and Mary Esther Huerta.
p. cm.
Includes bibliographical references and index.
ISBN 978-1-4166-1272-8 (pbk.: alk. paper) 1. Hispanic Americans—Education. 2. English language—Study and teaching—Spanish speakers—United States. 3. Education—Parent participation—United States. I. Delgado, Rocio. II. Huerta, Mary Esther. III. Title.
LC2686.4.C36 2011
371.829'68073—dc22

2011010754

20 19 18 17 16 15 14 13 12 11   1 2 3 4 5 6 7 8 9 10 11 12

To my father, Agapito D. Campos, who dreamed his sons would work far from the crop fields in which he labored.

—David

Para Fer, mis padres y nuestras familias; por compartir sus historias conmigo.

—Rocio

To my parents, Tony Soto and Ana María Carrasco Soto, whose foresight illuminated their children's education paths.

—Mary Esther

This text emerged from an interdependent and collaborative effort among the authors, who equally shared their lived experiences, talents, and creativity to advocate for Latino students.

REACHING OUT TO LATINO FAMILIES OF ENGLISH LANGUAGE LEARNERS

Foreword

R*eaching Out to Latino Families of English Language Learners* is published at a time when Latino children across the United States are increasingly attending public schools. Latino schoolchildren share certain characteristics: Most of them were born in the United States, and most are raised in households where Spanish is spoken. Educators cannot underestimate how each child's cultural and linguistic background influences the contexts of learning at home and school.

Ser padre Latino es un orgullo (I am proud to be a Latino parent). The most significant contribution that my husband, Armando, and I have given to our families is our children—Marisol, 9; Rodrigo, 8; and Miguel, 19 months. The pride that we feel develops from our family values, and particularly from the value we place on children. *Los niños son el orgullo del hogar* (children are the pride of our home)—particularly those who are educated. Growing up in Mexico, I came from a very strict but loving background where education was the norm. If we were involved in education, then we were our parents' pride. My mother was very involved in the schools in Mexico because she was very proud of her daughters and because the schools would reach out to her because of her talents (cooking and sewing); my father, who was an *obrero* (labor worker), worked all day, and the first thing he asked when he got home was, "*¿Terminaron la tarea?*" (Did you finish your homework?). When we moved to the United States, my parents were not involved in the schools primarily due to the language barrier. Educators didn't reach out to them because they didn't know how to work with Spanish-speaking immigrant families.

This book helps readers understand that educators can use Spanish to help build a foundation for creating strong home–school partnerships with the families of Latino

English language learners. I was 12 years old when my parents immigrated to the United States from Mexico. I entered middle school in the 1980s, an era when linguistic accommodations were rare in Texas and when Mexican immigrants were widely considered to be undocumented. I succeeded at school because of the support system I received from my parents, who only speak Spanish. Thirty years later, experiences such as my own are still common. *Reaching Out to Latino Families of English Language Learners* offers a unique range of guiding principles and ideas that school communities can explore, apply, and adapt based on their particular needs and goals for involving Latino parents at school. This book adds to our understanding of how effective school partnerships increase different types of parental involvement that enhance the academic success of Latino schoolchildren.

Mari Riojas Cortez, Ph.D.
Professor of Early Childhood Education
University of Texas at San Antonio

Introduction: Why Reaching Out Matters

The United States is becoming increasingly diverse. Federal census data indicate that 16 percent of the population (32.3 million people out of 200 million) in 1966 consisted of African, Latino, and Asian Americans (Pew Hispanic Center, 2006a). By 2006 that percentage had increased to 32.7 percent (97.7 million out of 300 million), not including the unauthorized/undocumented migrant population, which has been estimated at 11 million (Pew Hispanic Center, 2006b). Latinos accounted for the highest growth rate in the 40-year period: 36 percent. In fact, in July 2005, Latinos became the largest minority group in the United States, making up the fifth-largest "Latino" nation in the world and including an increasing population of young people. Federal data currently project that by July 2050, the U.S. Latino population will reach 102.6 million. By then, one in four Americans will be of Latino origin (Tomás Rivera Policy Institute, 2004).

The largest Latino groups in the United States are of Mexican, Puerto Rican, and Cuban heritage (Pérez & Torres-Guzmán, 2002). Most schoolchildren who speak languages other than English at home live in Arizona, California, Florida, Illinois, New Jersey, New Mexico, New York, and Texas (García, 2009). Furthermore, the 2000 Census estimated that there were nearly 9.8 million bilingual speakers ages 5 to 17. Of these, almost 70 percent speak Spanish at home.

What are the implications of these data for school practitioners? They underscore the fact that school practitioners will be teaching more Latino schoolchildren than ever before. By 2025, we can expect an additional 5.2 million children attending

U.S. schools, and 93 percent will be Latinos (Schmidt, 2005). Depending on the extent of overall integration with the mainstream culture and generational factors, many of these Latino youth may become acculturated by then; that is, they may have an enhanced understanding of values, beliefs, and behavior associated with middle-class American life. Nevertheless, many Latinos will need support navigating through the U.S. educational system, especially newcomers or recent immigrant students and their families.

This will be particularly true for English learners, whose numbers have increased dramatically over the last few decades. Between 1979 and 2006, the overall number of English learners increased from 3.8 million to 10.8 million (National Center for Education Statistics, 2008). Large urban school districts such as New York City Public Schools, Chicago Public Schools, and the Los Angeles Unified School District experienced the largest increases, with students speaking over a hundred different languages; but smaller school districts had sharp increases as well. Data for the 2003–04 school year show that services for English learners were provided to 3.8 million students, or 11 percent of all students (National Center for Education Statistics, 2006). Of this population, 80 percent were Latinos who reported that Spanish was their native language (National Council of La Raza, 2007). Data for 2005 revealed that of the Latino youth living in the United States, nearly a third reported that they spoke only English, half of this group reported that they spoke English very well, and 20 percent of the group indicated that they spoke English with limited proficiency.

With more Latinos, including English learners, in U.S. classrooms, it is important for teachers and administrators to become knowledgeable about and skillful in working with these students and their parents. Federal data suggest that schools currently are not fully meeting the particular academic needs of Latinos. For instance, Latinos—

- Are significantly less likely to complete high school. Latinos have the highest dropout rate nationwide—28 percent, which is double the rate of African Americans and four times that of their white peers. Only 48 percent of Latino males graduate from high school, and foreign-born Latinos account for more than 25 percent of all dropouts in the nation (National Council of La Raza, 2007).
- Have the least amount of education when compared to other major groups. Only 11 percent of those 25 or older have a bachelor's degree. Forty percent of Latino adults have not completed high school, and one out of four has less than a 9th grade education.

- Have low rates of enrollment in college-preparatory courses. Latinos are less likely to enroll in rigorous academic courses that prepare them for higher education. Although most Latino students are interested in pursuing challenging courses, fewer than half attend schools that offer such courses (National Council of La Raza, 2007).
- Are more likely to perform below grade level. Some studies reveal an average gap of more than 20 percentage points on high-stakes reading and math tests between Latinos and their white counterparts, for all age groups (American Federation of Teachers, 2004).

An undeniable factor that affects a child's school achievement is socioeconomic status. Children living in poverty may (1) live in substandard housing, which makes it difficult to find a suitable place to do homework; (2) lack the resources to access educational materials or experiences, such as visiting museums, zoos, or theaters, which limits opportunities for developing the background knowledge emphasized by schooling; (3) have limited or no access to adequate health care, which means that they may enter school without having their sight, hearing, speech, or other medical problems attended to; and (4) have poor nutrition. All these factors affect school performance, and here too the statistics are grim for Latinos: nearly one in three Latino infants is born into poverty (Children's Defense Fund, 2007).

Because social and economic factors often dictate availability and location of housing, many Latinos with low socioeconomic status live in isolated, low-income communities. Although more than half of Latino students speak primarily English at home, the effects of living in such communities are that many will speak English with limited proficiency, have few opportunities to interact with native speakers of English, and have little access to quality early-childhood programs. Although living in isolation can help preserve cultural values, beliefs, and practices, these may be incongruent with the culture of schools. For example, culture will influence child-rearing practices, work ethics, educational aspirations, and the way self-esteem is promoted and initiative is inspired. What is always important to keep in mind is that parents' level of education and socioeconomic background do not dictate a child's potential for succeeding in school. Thousands of Latinos have surmounted countless barriers and setbacks to become successful citizens who continue to make admirable contributions to society. Nevertheless, millions have also been left behind.

A quality education can offer children living in poverty opportunities leading to a stable economic future, and teachers at all levels make vital contributions that increase the likelihood of Latino students' academic success. Teachers can assume more responsibility to counter the social and economic barriers Latino youth encounter throughout their schooling. Excellent resources devoted to enhancing the academic and social achievement of Latino youth at school are already available. For example, ASCD has an excellent line of resources that help school practitioners design differentiated, meaningful, and rigorous instruction. These include *Classroom Instruction That Works with English Language Learners*; *Getting Started with English Language Learners: How Educators Can Meet the Challenge*; *Strategies for Success with English Language Learners: An ASCD Action Tool*; *Meeting the Needs of English Language Learners*; and *Research-Based Methods of Reading Instruction for English Language Learners: Grades 4–12*. All of these are ideal for teachers of English language learners.

This book focuses on strategies to increase the school engagement of Latino parents. We believe parents wield considerable power, because they not only provide their children's basic needs; they also influence their children's performance in school as they teach, guide, encourage, shape, counsel, nurture, and support them. Additionally, parents know their children's interests, strengths, weaknesses, aspirations, preferences, and aversions, which makes them ideal sources of information to tap when designing differentiated instruction.

We, the authors, share common backgrounds. We have a Mexican heritage, we are English learners, and we are teachers. Though we write through the perspective of our Mexican heritage, we honor the parallels and interactions that exist among Latino cultural groups. Our goal is to share our knowledge about the Latino culture and offer helpful ideas that promote parental involvement. We strongly believe that the more teachers understand the Latino culture, the better prepared they are to engage, build trust, and strengthen existing partnerships with parents.

In *Reaching Out to Latino Families of English Language Learners*, children and their parents are the central focus of each idea. We believe that parents are vital stakeholders in their child's educational journey and that it is important to discuss the power that schools hold in implementing the changes needed to increase Latino parental involvement. Therefore we discuss school policies, as well as societal and economic challenges. Our rationale for writing this book is to broaden perceptions and present divergent possibilities for engagement by parents, students, and teachers at all levels.

Implementing change requires mutual trust, creativity, innovation, and collaboration between partners. Moreover, each campus must establish goals and desired outcomes related to parental involvement. These goals and expected outcomes will dictate the process of change. At stake is the achievement of English language learners.

The chapters are designed to help teachers gain a holistic view of Latino parents and their children and to provide insight into the different contexts (home, school, and community) that influence their everyday lives. We hope to guide the development of an understanding of how culture influences learning, communication, and relationship building, so that readers will be inspired to proceed with confidence in reaching out to Latino parents.

1

A Critical Reflection: Exploring Self and Culture

The Latino culture is vibrant and complex. Differences within it are influenced by where people live, socioeconomic backgrounds, levels of education, religion, and individual lived experiences. These factors influence how people view and read their world (Gee, 1996; Vygotsky, 1986). As mentioned in the Introduction, we, the authors of this book, are Mexican Americans. Although we share a common heritage, we have different cultural backgrounds and practices that provide us with a unique perspective. Similarly, we ask you, our readers, to examine the experiences that contribute to your own worldview, which includes assumptions and perceptions about Latinos and their culture.

Exploring the Latino culture should begin with an introspective approach. When you take an authentic look at yourself, you begin to understand issues of diversity and become amenable to other points of view. This chapter begins with fundamental questions to guide your understanding of self and follows with a discussion of the variations within the Latino culture.

Taking a Personal Journey

Understanding diversity is a journey that begins at a personal level. Before exploring cultural dynamics and group differences, it is important to examine your unique worldview, which includes assumptions and perceptions. To recognize your own individual differences, consider, for example, the diversity within your family. How different are you from your siblings? How different are you from your parents? How different is your family in comparison to relatives? Exploring these kinds of questions is an initial step in the ongoing effort to develop cultural awareness.

Diversity exists within any cultural group. Even within the white population we see diverse ethnic subgroups (for example, people of German, Irish, or French heritage) whose members maintain and express particular valued cultural practices. These cultural expressions vary based on lived experiences related to such factors as geography, age, religion, and socioeconomic status. Therefore, we urge you to avoid making generalizations based on unexamined assumptions and perceptions that can sustain stereotypes. Overgeneralizations can result from limited or superficial assessments of observed behaviors and practices.

We urge teachers of English language learners to develop self-knowledge by gaining awareness of their "social positioning"—that is, their own power and privilege in relation to others. This is a pivotal step toward gaining respect, acceptance, and equity for groups that have been marginalized by schooling practices. Understanding one's worldview and social positioning engenders curiosity, inquiry, and interest about different cultural groups. In daily instruction, cultural awareness encompasses learning how to build meaningful connections with students and their families. For instance, a teacher's willingness to explore the rearing practices of an African American family, the discipline methods of a Hmong parent, and the dietary habits of a Hindu family exemplifies purposeful cultivation of both cultural and self-awareness. Thus, interest in learning about students helps the teacher design and deliver authentic learning experiences while enhancing cultural sensitivity.

Learning about diversity entails a movement from self-awareness to inquiry to action through advocacy for students who are marginalized by the educational system. In the context of this book, we define *advocacy* as the act of creating equitable opportunities for Latino parents of English language learners to strengthen their engagement as key stakeholders in their child's schooling.

As you read this book, consider the following questions to guide your journey in understanding Latino parents of English language learners:

- *What kinds of interactions have you had with the Latino culture?* Think about the context in which you have interacted with Latinos. Were these formal or informal interactions? Were these conversations or one-way communication? What did you talk about? Who did most of the talking? What were your observations during these interactions?

- *What have you heard about the Latino culture?* Often, informal conversations, including sayings and jokes, may engender and reinforce stereotypes about the Latino culture. Although these stereotypes may be unintentional and lighthearted, be aware that they are never inconsequential.
- *What observations have you made about the Latino culture?* How do your worldviews, assumptions, or perceptions about Latinos influence these observations? Consider how social factors—for example, socioeconomic status, age, gender, race/ethnicity—can influence your observations. Also, think about whether your responses are based on a single observation or any misinformation. Critical reflection through questioning is at the core of eliminating stereotypes.
- *What messages do the media communicate about the Latino culture?* Consider how the media, such as sitcoms and other TV shows, magazines, and virtual media, represent the Latino culture and how these images influence your perceptions of the Latino way of life. A discerning person recognizes that the Latino culture is heterogeneous and that media portrayals are frequently based on generalizations and stereotypes.
- *How do your background and lived experiences influence your understanding of diverse cultures?* Consider your interactions with diverse populations. Traveling to different countries, visiting local cultural centers, and interacting with individuals from diverse cultures can broaden your understanding of how individuals across the globe navigate life. These are opportunities that can enrich your school community. Moreover, students, parents, and communities represent vital resources that you can tap into to learn about the Latino culture.

As you forge new pathways in your journey, we suggest that you keep these critical reflections in mind. The information you gain will nurture your ability to accept and learn about divergent ways of thinking, of interacting with schools, and of expressing what Nel Noddings (2002) has called an "ethic of care," a concept that we cover in detail in Chapter 2.

Recognizing Language Differences

Many Latinos speak two languages, Spanish and English, and this situation is more complex than one might imagine. It is important to understand that Latinos may not be the same linguistically even if they speak the same language or dialect (Gutiérrez-Clellen, Calderón, & Weismer, 2004). For example, two Latina teachers who were team-teaching a student cohort experienced this phenomenon when one reported to the other that the students had not followed her directions when she asked them to put on their coats before going out. Mrs. Castro, who is originally from Guatemala, explained that she had given the following instructions: "*Les he pedido a los patojos que se pongan las chumpas.*" Ms. Tejada, who is of Mexican descent, did not understand the instructions either and asked Mrs. Castro to explain what she intended to say. Both teachers agreed that the reason the students (who were also of Mexican heritage) had not followed directions was because they were not familiar with the vocabulary that Mrs. Castro used. The children used different words for "children" and "coats." The teachers decided to use this as a learning opportunity to enrich their students' Spanish vocabulary and to help them learn English. Mrs. Castro and Ms. Tejada brainstormed a list of Spanish words that have similar meanings in different Latin American countries and provided English translations to their students:

- Words for "children": *patojos, huercos, niños, chilpayates, huache*
- Words for "coat, jacket": *chumpa, chamarra, chaqueta, sobretodo, abrigo*

Although both Spanish and English are *alphabetic* languages (that is, they use an alphabet to represent words, unlike a nonalphabetic language, such as Chinese), each is a distinct language system. Each has its separate cueing system, which includes phonology (sounds), semantics (word meanings), syntax (grammatical structure), and pragmatics (social and culturally appropriate use of language). Additionally, each Spanish-speaking community displays variations within each of these language cueing systems. For example, note these differences in how a Spanish-speaking person may ask a simple question such as "What do you want?" A person of Puerto Rican heritage may ask, "*¿Qué tu quieres?*" Someone of Mexican heritage will structure the same question differently: "*¿Qué quieres?*" Each person's speech production will also vary in speed, intonation, inflection (phonology), and other marked characteristics.

Spanish and English have other differences in language structure. For example, English has 44 *phonemes* (the smallest unit of sound in a language) represented by 26 letters, but Spanish phonemes vary between 22 and 24, depending on whether the language is spoken in the U.S. Southwest, Latin America, or Spain (Pérez & Torres-Guzmán, 2002). Also, Spanish is considered a "transparent" language because it has a close letter-to-sound correspondence, which is not the case with English. These examples enable us to view language as a cultural tool and provide insight about the heterogeneity among Latino speech communities.

Understanding Cultural Practices

The construction of culture occurs within family units through caretakers. Over time, children learn the language, traditions, attitudes, behaviors, and institutions associated with their culture. The intimate languages shared among caretakers and young children are known as "primary discourses," and these facilitate the learning of cultural rules and norms particular to children's speech communities (Brisk & Harrington, 2007) and how they use language and literacy (Heath, 1983). Children who grow up in a bilingual environment also understand the distinctiveness of the cultures in which they function (García, 2009).

Celebrations further highlight distinctiveness among Latino cultures. Many Mexican Americans in the southwestern United States, for example, celebrate Easter by decorating *cascarones,* which are a variation of the plastic Easter egg common to mainstream culture. *Cascarones* are colorfully decorated eggshells filled with confetti. On Easter Sunday, the fragile *cascarones* are hidden, and an egg hunt ensues. After collecting the *cascarones,* children crack them over their loved ones' heads in a celebratory gesture. This cultural expression may not be practiced in other Latino communities, which may celebrate Easter by attending church services or sharing a meal with family members; and some may not observe Easter at all.

Food is another expression of distinctiveness. Fried plantains, for example, are generally found in Cuban and Puerto Rican American cuisine but are not common among other Latinos. Teachers can use these distinct features within Latino communities as vehicles for learning more about the cultures of students in the classroom. For example, when studying about indigenous civilizations, a 3rd grade teacher encouraged her students' families to share edible products that they—like the Aztecs and the Mayans—made from corn. Students learned about Colombian *arepas,* Salvadoran *pupusas,* and Mexican *gorditas* and discussed similarities and differences among these dishes from Latin American countries and their ancient civilizations.

Learning About Students' Cultural Background

The variations in Latino culture underscore why it is important to learn about students' backgrounds rather than making assumptions, and learning about students' lived experiences is easier if you establish a partnership with each family. Getting to know each student as an individual enables you to do the following:

- Communicate effectively with parents once you find out how parents and children self-identify.
- Begin instruction by integrating students' prior knowledge gained at home and at school.
- Access background information from parents regarding their children's interests, aspirations, strengths, and weaknesses to design instruction that scaffolds their current knowledge.
- Choose teaching strategies that complement the styles and preferences for learning that individual students make apparent.
- Facilitate an understanding among your students about how diversity begins at home and occurs among family members.
- Validate all students' heritage. This can be done by providing learning opportunities that enable all students to learn about many cultures. Intentional planning of multicultural content is an additive approach that includes everyone as a learner, and deep learning experiences enable students to explore how diversity sustains democratic principles.

In sum, the more you know about each student, the more insight you gain not only about the Latino cultures represented in your classroom but also about the range of student abilities, knowledge, interests, and areas where growth is needed. All serve to inform your instruction and to build relationships with parents. With academic success as the communicated shared goal, parents will likely be motivated to support the learning goals and objectives that you establish.

An example of how strengthening home-to-school connections can improve instruction comes from the experience of a 3rd grade teacher, Mrs. Williams, who took a proactive step by making a home visit to learn more about one of her students, Mario. Although she had been providing Mario with ample direct, explicit instruction to support his work in math, he was not making significant progress. When she visited her student's home, Mrs. Williams observed how Mario learned vicariously and through modeling. She noticed that when Mario and his dad were working on the family car, his father used one-word commands and wordless gestures. Drawing inferences from implicit information, Mario intuitively understood his father's intents. Mrs. Williams discovered from speaking to Mario's mother that he did not have previous experience working on cars; however, Mrs. Williams had observed how he performed successfully as an apprentice to his father. In this scenario, the teacher gained deep insight about her student, including different approaches to solving problems, multimodal uses of communication, and how family values influenced teaching and learning preferences.

Other ways to learn about individual students' cultural background include using students as resources, creating project-based assignments, conducting focus group meetings with parents, spending time in the community, reading about Latino culture, and using Spanish-language media. We briefly discuss these approaches here because all are essential components in any consideration of ways to familiarize yourself with the Latino culture. We also discuss them in greater detail in subsequent chapters to guide systematic implementation.

Use Students as Resources

Latino students can be a direct source of information that enriches your understanding of the Latino culture. For example, to prepare students to write about one of their cultural celebrations, you could invite older students to discuss and answer questions about such events. Students can share information about particular cultural values and beliefs by telling stories, explaining rites of passage, and describing ceremonies associated with celebrations.

For example, a Mexican American *quinceañera* is a celebration, similar to a debutante ball, that inducts a young girl into society, marking a transition into womanhood on her 15th birthday. Some of the Latino students in your classroom may be familiar with this cultural event and will draw connections between their lived experiences when completing their writing assignment. In one Texas school, 4th grade students were working on writing descriptive essays about a family event. Esmeralda decided to write about her sister's *quinceañera*. The teacher understood the value of using students' experiences as resources and invited Esmeralda's sister to speak to the class. The sister shared highlights of the festivities and answered questions about this important family event. By taking this approach, the teacher gained personal insight about this celebration and created an opportunity for her students to write about a culturally relevant topic, which sparked their interest and engaged them as writers.

Another approach might entail establishing casual and ongoing dialogues with upper-grade students during recess, in the hallways, or during club meetings. Mrs. Ruiz was talking to students on the playground one day when Guillermo mentioned that he bought a kite at the *pulga* (flea market) over the weekend. As he excitedly described his prized acquisition, Mrs. Ruiz asked him to tell her more, which enhanced this particular student's communicative abilities. This informal conversation also boosted Guillermo's self-esteem and motivated him to converse more frequently. After surveying the students who had been to the *pulga*, Mrs. Ruiz created instructional connections in math by guiding students to create various graphs using the survey results. She also helped them brainstorm ideas about items they had acquired at the *pulga* or visits they had made there with their families to guide their writing about the topic during language arts instruction.

Create Project-Based Assignments

Project-based assignments that involve students in conducting research about their own heritage can become effective ways to show that you value cultural diversity within the school setting. Obviously it is important to always proceed with empathy and sensitivity. Some families may be unwilling to participate, especially if they are undocumented immigrants, have sought political asylum, or are war refugees. If it is feasible to proceed, however, children will engage and develop important academic skills as they conduct research and interview their parents, grandparents, and other community members. As a schoolwide effort, students can share completed projects through cultural fairs, panel presentations, performances, participation in focus group discussions, cuisine parties, fashion shows, dances, and games.

Student projects can also involve researching famous Latinos. By conducting web quests or web searches on the Internet to retrieve information on well-known figures, students engage in learning opportunities that value the many positive contributions of Latinos. The possibilities are numerous, and the following list is by no means all-inclusive: actors Rita Moreno, Anthony Quinn, Ricardo Montalbán, Ricardo Antonio Chavira, and Hector Elizondo; writers Sandra Cisneros, Alberto Baltazar Urista Heredia, and Reinaldo Arenas; social activitists César Chávez, Dolores Huerta, Judy Baca, and Martin Espada; musicians Jerry and Andy Gonzalez, Juan Luis Guerra, and Lalo Guerrero; politicians Henry B. Gonzales, Bill Richardson, and Henry Cisneros; artists David Diaz, Laura Aguilar, and Carlos Almaraz; Nobel Prize winners Mario Molina and Severo Ochoa; astronauts Ellen Ochoa and Franklin R. Chang-Diaz; dancer Fernando Bujones; athletes Henry Cejudo, Rebecca Lobo, Roberto Clemente, Nancy Lopez, and Lee Trevino; and playwright María Irene Fornés. Other possibilities include regional and local leaders who may be familiar to students.

Conduct Focus Group Meetings

Another way you can learn about the cultural background of your students is to conduct focus group meetings where key stakeholders engage in participatory dialogue. Focus group meetings typically consist of small groups guided by a facilitator who asks thoughtful questions to elicit meaningful information. A focus group may be composed of your students' parents as well as parents of students in other grades. In the spirit of preparing for the meeting, ask other teachers or members of your campus leadership team to recommend reliable school workers or school volunteers to share valuable information with you about your students' Latino heritage. To ensure that the meeting is worthwhile, consider the following suggestions:

- *Start each meeting with clearly stated purposes and goals.* Here are some possible opening statements: "This meeting is about getting to know each other." "This is a time to learn how each of us can help your child succeed in school." "I hope to learn and also share ideas about how to support your children and their studies." "I know that parents are a child's first teachers."
- *Ask questions that will provide you the most benefit*—for example, questions about customs generally associated with Latino cultures. Questions about matters such as immigration status, politics, or sexuality are inappropriate; not only are these sensitive topics that have no immediate bearing on your instruction, but they also will immediately embarrass parents and perhaps turn them away from schools for good. You could start off with "Would you mind if I asked you some questions about your culture?" and lead to "What do you want people to know about your culture?"
- *Invite a community leader.* Ask the parents or the children to identify a person in the community whom they hold in high regard. Consider asking church leaders, a city council representative, a member of the Hispanic Chamber of Commerce, directors of cultural centers, or representatives of other such community entities. Most leaders would embrace the opportunity to share their perspectives.

Because communication is fundamental to conducting a successful focus group meeting, it is important to have a translator/interpreter on hand at all times. Reproducible A.1 in Appendix A provides helpful Spanish words to use when communicating with parents who do not understand a vocabulary word commonly associated with school. Additionally, you can make copies of the reproducible for parents as a handy reference for terms associated with instruction, classrooms, and schools.

Explore the Community

A good way to better understand the social and cultural background of your students is to explore their community. A first step might involve reflecting upon the items outlined in Figure 1.1, which can guide your exploration of the particular background and lived experiences of the Latino families in the community. More important, this reflective process can begin to challenge any existing preconceptions as you identify the diversity among Latinos. The next step is to drive around the Latino community to locate shopping areas, entertainment venues, churches, and social service agencies and institutions. You can also learn about the community by shopping at local grocery stores. For example, south-central Texas has two grocery chains that cater to Latinos—La Michoacana and Fiesta. Many grocery stores sell Spanish-language newspapers, magazines, and other publications (for example, *La Prensa* and *El Mundo*) that convey community perspectives regarding politics, social affairs, and pop culture. Many Latino families also shop at flea markets or swap meets, where they can barter or negotiate for reduced prices for items including fruits and vegetables, new clothing, home fixtures, and home repair materials, as well as decorative goods and sundries from their country of origin.

FIGURE 1.1

Learning About Your School's Families

1. Describe the location of the school (within the state, city, neighborhood; urban or rural area).
2. What are some of the benefits and challenges associated with your school's location?
3. Use this table as a guide to learn about the Latino families in your school community.

What	Why
Find out whether the Latino families live in isolation (separate from one another) or in an area that is predominately Latino.	Because geographical/regional factors may influence language use or accessibility of resources within the community.
Find out whether the Latino children share a home with their parents, grandparents, aunts, uncles, and other caretakers.	Because some Latino families are composed of nuclear and extended family members who can play an important role in the child's schooling.
Find out how the Latino parents identify themselves (e.g., Latino, Mexican, Mexican American, Chicano, Hispanic, and so on).	Because Latinos identify themselves in many ways.
Find out the family's socioeconomic status (SES) (e.g., free, reduced-, or full-price lunch).	Because SES is a component of diversity that suggests levels of opportunities and choices in a child's social and academic life.
Find out the level of educational attainment of each parent.	Because many Latino parents have completed high school and beyond, they are literate and can support your instruction (for example, by reading to the class).
Find out how the Latino parents communicate about education to their children.	Because all parents want their children to experience educational success, parents can share best approaches for teaching their child.

Businesses within the community can be potential sites for field trips. Bakeries (*panaderías*) and ice cream shops (*paleterías* or *neverías*) may offer students and teachers unique learning experiences. For example, you could use a trip to the *panadería* (bakery) to provide background for teaching the children vocabulary (for example, words such as "oven," "ingredients"); reading about pastries from all over the world; teaching a math lesson about measurement, quantity, and time; and teaching a science lesson recording changes in size, mass, and color that result from baking at a certain temperature.

Community celebrations, which are often held in city parks or other public facilities, can be integrated with social studies instruction. Check local events calendars to find out information. Some ethnic-based festivities include Cinco de Mayo (May 5), Puerto Rico's Constitution Day (July 25), Cuba's birth as an independent republic (May 20), and Día de los Muertos (November 1 and 2). Visiting community church services offers the opportunity to learn about community creeds, values, and ideologies.

Also consider having lunch or dinner with a student's family at a local restaurant. Sharing a meal is another opportunity to learn about the family's history and culture by way of observation and genuine conversation. This type of interaction can lessen anxiety as parents begin to see you outside of school. If parents perceive you as an ally and advocate for their child, this perception could spark their interest in getting involved at school.

Well-planned home visits are also valuable. Students may not make a banner and openly declare their appreciation for your home visits, but most likely they and their parents will interpret your willingness to reach out as a positive act.

The Internet offers another way to familiarize yourself with the Latino culture. This tool allows you to locate cultural centers, museums, public libraries, churches, private schools, factories, and other entities within the community. Most cities have their own website and web-based versions of newspapers listing weekly entertainment and cultural activities. Chicago, for instance, has a webpage with buttons linked to "Things to See and Do" and "Neighborhoods." One link will even retrieve information on the colorful murals located in the predominantly Latino neighborhoods. Even smaller cities have websites with links to calendars of events. And don't overlook other, more general websites devoted to the Latino culture, which can further your understanding and provide information that you can work into daily instruction (see Appendix B).

Your engagement in the community, along with the relationships you establish, can enable you to deliver culturally responsive instruction as you connect school learning to children's lives outside of school. All of these suggestions for exploring the community are intended to offer ideas and artifacts that can make lessons more informative, relevant, and meaningful to students. In addition, if parents witness your respectful efforts to participate in their community, they are more likely to reciprocate by viewing their involvement in the school in positive ways. Chapter 7 has more information on making connections with the community and forging partnerships.

Read About Latino Culture

Books can be an important source of information about Latino culture, history, and peoples. Culturally authentic books—both fiction and nonfiction—are worth reading and sharing with all your students. A critical attribute of "authentic" children's literature is the inclusion of themes and characters that accurately represent the culture. This means that narratives contain content that represents the culture and characters in authentic ways, have rich plots, and use language accurately. Authentic literature about Latinos avoids stereotypical themes and characters and generic plots and settings. Look for lists of books that have won the Américas Award for Children's and Young Adult Literature, the Pura Belpré Award, and the Tomás Rivera Children's Book Award. Appendix C lists a number of books that are worth reading for background information or as sources of literary works.

Tap into Spanish-Language Media

Even though you may not know Spanish, consider tuning in to Univision to watch the news or other programming. Often individuals learning Spanish watch soap operas to learn Spanish words and phrases. More important, watching Spanish-language programs may help you bond with your students (and their parents), especially when you mention some of the shows they watch. Imagine how thrilled your students will be when you rely on their expertise to answer the question that you pose: "Last night I watched the *noticias* on channel 41 and the newscaster used the word ____. What does that mean?" You could make a game of it and mention to them that you are planning to watch a particular show and will try to closely follow the unfolding of events but will need their help to fully understand the characters, the plot, and so forth. Then, have students explain all the nuances that made little sense to you.

Also, consider watching Spanish-language movies with English subtitles. Many of the popular movies (for example, *Como Agua Para Chocolate, Bajo la Misma Luna,*

Conejo en la Luna, Al Otro Lado, Diarios de Motocicleta, Un Día sin Mexicanos, Buscando a Leti, El Cometa, Gringuito, Casi Casi, Women on the Verge of a Nervous Breakdown, El Norte, Maria Full of Grace, The Other Conquest) are available on DVD. These films will increase your awareness of cultural distinctiveness. When the content is appropriate, you can use Spanish-language media as conversation starters with your students or their parents. Spanish radio and music could be used in similar fashion. Consider listening to regional music and learning the lyrics of songs by pop artists such as Mark Anthony, Jennifer Lopez, Enrique Iglesias, and Gloria Estefan. You can casually mention that you learned a Spanish song but need students' expertise in helping you understand the content, particular lyrics, and the images they convey.

All of these activities have the same goal: to learn more about your students and your school community. This is an important first step toward gaining the understanding you need to reach out to Latino parents and encourage their participation in their children's education.

TAKE **ACTION**

- Read historical references to learn about the sociocultural variations of Latino cultures.
- Read professional articles associated with second-language acquisition and learning.
- Ask those who have learned a second language to share their experiences.
- Visit informally with parents to learn how the native language is used at home and in the community.
- Learn key vocabulary to facilitate casual communication with parents.
- Learn about the cultural activities and holidays that your students' families celebrate.
- Identify community outlets, sites, and institutions that your students' families frequent.
- Locate community centers and attend cultural events (for example, concerts and theater performances) that focus on the Latino culture.

2

Engaging Latino Parents Through an Ethic of Care

In this chapter, we take the discussion beyond the cultural traits of Latinos and encourage you to think about how your school community responds to Latino parents and their engagement at school. To that end, we recommend that schools shift their perspective of how they view Latino parental engagement by considering a bottom-up instead of a top-down approach. Schools can then begin to identify and listen to the voiced needs of the Latino parent community to encourage systemic change. The discussion focuses on promoting an ethic of care toward Latino parents—that is, valuing the role of parents as key stakeholders throughout their child's academic journey.

Respecting Cultural Variations

Culture is dynamic, and Latino parents display a variety of cultural practices. Like all parents, some will seem more social than others, some may have a more direct demeanor than others, and some may demand explicit information about the instruction you provide. These differences emerge from lived experiences and worldviews (Pérez, 2004). In other words, particular life experiences (for example, child-rearing practices, social exchanges, schooling) influence individual expression and behavior, as does context. These differences may be expressed in various ways. For example, in a social setting such as a PTA (or PTO) meeting, some Latino parents may perceive and use space differently than others. They may sit or stand in closer proximity than what is considered acceptable by mainstream culture. In personal exchanges, some Latino parents may use physical touch, such as shaking your hand or patting you on the shoulder or back, to establish familiarity, an important facet of relationship building for Latinos. One classroom teacher recalled being surprised when a student's mother sat very close to her during a parent–teacher conference. The mother joked about a comment that her son had made as she nudged the teacher's forearm. The intent was to establish familiarity with the teacher and acknowledge their common connection to the child.

Although cultural expressions may vary, any parent will welcome a warm greeting and appreciate casual and friendly exchanges. Moreover, conveying a low level of stress through demeanor and expression when conversing with Latino parents may encourage ongoing dialogues over time.

Brief but frequent interactions with parents can prove to be important ways to understand their varying ideas, viewpoints, and perceptions. Consider that Latino parents are as heterogeneous as their children. As a parent–teacher relationship grows, teachers can gauge how and when to progressively ask parents key questions about their role in their child's schooling. Of course, all questions should be asked with sensitivity (for a list of possible questions to spur conversations with parents, see Chapter 3).

Latino parents may also differ in the way they participate at school. Some will be highly interested and engaged in their child's learning, whereas others may seem distant or uninterested. Take a reflective stance when you notice yourself making any negative assumptions about a parent's interest in his or her child's schooling. Beyond reflection, seek opportunities for frequent, rich conversations with parents to draw more equitable, unbiased, and objective assessments about any particular circumstances. Generally, parents want their child to succeed academically, regardless of ethnicity, social class, or level of education (Nieto, Bode, & Bode, 2007), despite media coverage that frequently reports on those few who are physically or emotionally abusive or neglect to provide basic necessities. A preponderance of such stories target ethnic minorities, portraying parents of particular ethnic groups as not caring about their children's welfare. According to Nieto and her colleagues, *all* parents understand and believe that education offers their child unique opportunities for future prospects.

Latino parents hold high expectations for their children. Consider that many families have intentionally immigrated to the United States to pursue improved life opportunities. Of course, the purposes for immigrating vary and range from escaping economic hardships to fleeing war or seeking political asylum. Many families have left behind loved ones and have traveled through and survived harsh conditions. For many, the journey to the United States required making sacrifices, being resourceful, and being courageous.

One middle school teacher in New Mexico shared what had taken place in a conference she conducted with a Latino father to discuss inappropriate student behavior. During the meeting, the father pleaded with the teacher for continued patience with his son. He explained that he did not want his son to have dirty hands. The teacher was perplexed at the comment and asked him to explain. The father, an auto mechanic, showed her his own hands, caked with oil and grease, and said, "*Yo no quiero que mi hijo tenga que ensuciarse las manos como yo cuando él trabaje. Quiero que siga adelante con la escuela para que tenga una vida mejor que la mía*" (I don't want my son to have to get his hands dirty like me when he works. I want him to go ahead and succeed in school so that he has a life better than mine). This Latino parent wanted his son to work in a white-collar profession and to prosper financially. Personal stories that communicate similar goals for children abound in Latino communities.

Expectations and Parental Engagement

Parents' engagement at school has been linked to improved academic outcomes for students. Research also indicates that the effects of parent engagement may vary across ethnicities. This means that mainstream schools' cultural expectations about parents' engagement may be mismatched with how each community of diverse ethnic groups, including Latinos, interprets involvement (Ramírez, 2003). It is important to remember that school success is facilitated when a child's linguistic and sociocultural background is congruent with schooling expectations. In other words, children whose parents have high levels of education, speak English, and maintain at least a middle-class socioeconomic status enjoy privileges associated with the U.S. school system.

Some of these privileges include knowing and understanding the language used for instruction, seeing familiar middle-class characteristics and icons in the curriculum, and being familiar with testing procedures. Keep in mind that these expectations may be incongruent with the experiences of children and families who live in poverty and come from culturally and linguistically diverse backgrounds. Parents and school-aged children who have recently immigrated from Mexico, for example, may be familiar with testing only through essay writing (and thus unfamiliar with the U.S. standardized testing system), with classroom settings that are only self-contained (and thus be challenged by having to transition from one classroom period to another throughout the instructional day), and with instruction that is only direct and explicit (and thus unfamiliar with constructivist-based methods such as inquiry-based instruction or cooperative-learning approaches to complete academic tasks).

Remember that countless factors influence Latino parent engagement. Parents who are recent immigrants may be unfamiliar with typical and expected forms of interaction at your school. Additional barriers that parents may encounter on a school campus include language, negative attitudes, or even racism. When parents feel excluded or unwelcomed, they become reluctant to participate in school activities, to respond to notices or phone calls, or to volunteer for the school's parent–teacher association, carnivals, or special committees, despite repeated invitations. When parents do not show up for back-to-school night or parent–teacher conferences, school personnel may interpret parents' behavior as indifference toward their children's schooling (Quiocho & Daoud, 2006).

Reticence in response to repeated invitations to become more involved may simply be the result of Latino parents having a different interpretation of parental involvement. They may believe that they are already doing everything in their power to prepare their youngsters for school when they make sure that the children are well fed, dressed, and rested and that they have their supplies. Additionally, Latino parents may define engagement as teaching children to work hard, to respect and mind the teacher, and to adhere to the educational aspirations that parents share about the importance of succeeding at school.

To address any incongruent perceptions about parental involvement, school personnel must proactively create an inviting community where everyone exudes a spirit that fosters a commitment to make parents feel respected, welcome, and supported and where behavior aligns with that spirit. This responsibility belongs to all school personnel because they wield the authority and power that the institution of schooling represents. How a school enacts community building in general frames a particular ethic of care for Latino parents and their children.

Valuing Social and Cultural Capital

To initiate an ethic of care, teachers and other school personnel must first consider the context (the community, philosophy of education, and authentic needs) that influences the daily lives of Latino families. The first step entails listening to the voiced needs of Latino parents and convincing them of their vital role in their child's education.

Noddings (2002) proposed that responsive schooling practices depend on listening to the voiced needs of the community and aligning school practices to support these. With this in mind, the school action plan should be guided by the fundamental goal of strengthening home-to-school connections. The two primary objectives of this aspect of the plan would be to become acquainted with parents and the school community served. Teachers can enhance their knowledge about what it is like to live in a particular community by identifying the existing resources available to parents and families, including the social capital and cultural capital represented in the Latino community. McLaren (2009) defines these terms:

- "Social capital" refers to the collectively owned economic and cultural capital of any ethnic group. The Latino community has particular social capital from which individuals benefit and receive support. For instance, a Latina mother may belong to a social, religious network known as *Guadalupanas* where group members raise funds for their church community. Additionally, group membership affords opportunities for exchanging information and services (e.g., child care, food preparation, references for medical care, etc.), which builds capacity in navigating daily life in the United States. These examples of group membership strengthen social connections, enhance networking, and build particular background.
- "Cultural capital" refers to the general cultural background, knowledge, disposition, and skills that are passed from one generation to another. Cultural capital includes notions about a "work ethic" as well as ways of talking and behaving, modes of socializing, valued forms of knowledge, values, and beliefs. In the Latino community, cultural capital may include multimodal communication styles (i.e., bilingualism, code-switching, and *caló* or U.S. Chicano Spanish slang). This creative, open-ended use of language has been found to lead to cognitive flexibility, enhanced linguistic repertoires, and community identity (Zentella, 1997).

Responsive schooling practices value children's social and cultural capital. One way to value social and cultural capital is by viewing these attributes as assets and by incorporating them in the learning events that children experience each day at school. Consider the possibilities available when you recognize and tap the social and cultural capital of the Latino students in your classroom. In preparation for a school performance, for example, an insightful teacher can contact a classroom mother who knows a seamstress who can sew skirts for the girls, a parent who knows about carpentry and will construct stage props, and another parent who can prepare Mexican pastries for refreshments. Social capital and cultural capital are pillars that help to support the Latino community, and valuing them represents another facet of an ethic of care.

Understanding Needs Through Organized Meetings

Listening to and respecting parents' input represents another pillar of the ethic of care. Typically, educational policies are crafted on the basis of parents' and students' inferred needs rather than on their expressed needs (Noddings, 2002). Ignoring the expressed needs of students, parents, and their community may lead to missed opportunities to form partnerships. Noddings provides the following criteria to help teachers distinguish between different types of needs. A "want" is an expressed need if it—

- Is stable and intense over time (for example, parents have aspirations for their children to be college-bound).
- Is connected to a desirable end, and the end cannot be reached without the want (for example, a mother wants a scholarship for her son to attend a summer math camp and needs his teacher's letter of support).
- Is in the power of those addressed to grant it (for example, a group of parents want to increase the number of crossing guards at a busy intersection near the school, and they petition the principal). In addition, the person wanting must be willing and able to contribute to satisfy the want.

The last point directly communicates the need for collaborative activity, which could support the establishment of partnerships (for example, a group of parents want to have after-school care at the school and form a cooperative to work with school personnel to create and operate a program).

How do you get parents to express their needs? Figure 2.1 shows a model for ongoing meetings that can guide the process of enabling parents. The model has three stages:

- Stage 1 is a teacher-directed meeting with a core group of Latino parents.
- Stage 2 involves teacher and parents sharing the responsibility of leading meetings.
- Stage 3 involves sharing increased responsibilities for subsequent meetings with a larger group of parents.

Although meetings at each stage are organized and structured, the content should be open-ended and determined by parents. Because teachers are knowledgeable about policies and procedures, their role is vital throughout the process to facilitate, clarify, provide information, and act as liaisons between parents and the school district.

For Stage 1, meet with a small group of parents as your core participants. The small-group format facilitates making decisions about the best times and dates for

FIGURE 2.1
Three Stages for Parent Meetings

<table>
<tr><th colspan="2">Stage 1: Teacher Directed, Core Group of Latino Parents</th></tr>
<tr><th>Agenda</th><th>Goals</th></tr>
<tr><td>Meeting 1: September; 45 minutes<ul><li>Meet and greet each other.</li><li>Meet one key school worker (e.g., school's parent volunteer coordinator, community liaison, social worker).</li><li>State purpose of this meeting.</li><li>Teacher initiates a conversation. Teacher must be able to manage communication and exchanges, especially when participants' views and opinions differ.</li><li>Teacher charts the information for next meeting.</li><li>Decide on a date, time, and location for the next meeting.</li></ul></td><td>Teacher posts the following goals:<ul><li>To establish a core group of parents.</li><li>To have parents enjoy a low-risk environment.</li><li>To engage parents in conversation about needs, questions, and concerns regarding school or their community.</li><li>To generate two needs/wants.</li><li>To communicate that different views are perceived as a learning opportunity.</li><li>To encourage each parent to recruit one parent for the following meeting.</li></ul></td></tr>
<tr><th colspan="2">Stage 2: Shared Responsibility</th></tr>
<tr><td>Meeting 2: November; time decided by group<ul><li>Meet and greet each other.</li><li>Meet a new school worker.</li><li>One or two parents volunteer to initiate conversation. They review the items addressed in the previous session for the group. Parents will add two items.</li><li>Teacher helps facilitate the conversation:<ul><li>Asks about or addresses needs/wants.</li><li>Charts the information for next meeting.</li></ul></li><li>Decide on a date, time, and location for the next meeting.</li></ul></td><td>(Two parents become group leaders.)<ul><li>To have parents help create a low-risk environment for new participants.</li><li>To continue to engage parents in conversation about needs, questions, and concerns regarding school or their community.</li><li>To add two additional needs/wants.</li><li>To have parents and teacher share ideas about how to meet needs/wants.</li><li>To have parents initiate conversation.</li></ul></td></tr>
<tr><th colspan="2">Stage 3: Increased Shared Responsibility</th></tr>
<tr><td>Meeting 3: February; time decided by group<ul><li>Meet and greet each other.</li><li>Discuss benefits of past two meetings.</li><li>Two new parents volunteer to initiate conversation. They review the items addressed in the previous session for the group. Parents will add two new items.</li><li>Teacher helps facilitate the conversation:<ul><li>Parents share ideas about how to meet or address needs/wants. Teacher contributes.</li><li>Group decides on a need for future meetings.</li></ul></li><li>Decide on a date, time, and location for the next meeting.</li></ul></td><td>(Two new parents become group leaders.)<ul><li>To have parents help create a low-risk environment.</li><li>To continue to engage parents in conversation about needs, questions, and concerns regarding school or their community, adding two needs/wants.</li><li>To have parents and teacher collaborate on how to meet needs/wants.</li><li>To have parents initiate conversation.</li></ul></td></tr>
</table>

follow-up meetings. This core group can be composed of Latino parents with whom you already have a strong rapport. Gathering a small group helps maintain focus on the goals and objectives of each meeting, which should target understanding Latino parents' expressed needs. Meeting with a small group also makes it easier to actually act on the suggestions and needs the parents may offer.

Serving light refreshments can inspire friendly conversation and contribute to a welcoming environment. Working with a Spanish-speaking colleague also helps to establish a low-stress, low-risk climate. The location of the meeting may be the classroom, another location on campus, a meeting room at the public library or community cultural center, or any location that is comfortable, accessible to parents, and conducive to the participants interacting with each other. The core group of parents can help recruit additional parents for subsequent meetings and can even assume leadership roles over time. Of course, it is important to keep in mind that any meetings held on the school campus must adhere to school policies that govern parent meetings.

Consider the following example of an outcome of a Stage 1 meeting and how it relates to the earlier discussion of Noddings's criteria for "wants" and "expressed needs." A parent of a child at a rural elementary school voiced her concern about the children's safety (the want must be stable and intense over time). The children had to walk to school in a high-traffic, high-speed zone that lacked signage. At the meeting, the parent voiced her need (the want was connected to a desirable end). In subsequent Stage 1 meetings, parents discussed the issue, brainstormed solutions, and gathered information about how to proceed. They also invited the principal to listen to their needs and inquired about the protocol to follow (the want is in the power of those addressed to grant it). This core group of parents generated a letter and presented it at a school board meeting (the person wanting is willing and able to contribute to satisfy the want), petitioning for an increased number of traffic signs along the school route. When parents later saw the signs posted, they understood their ability to make desirable changes for the benefit of all children.

In Stage 2 meetings, each member of the core group is charged with the responsibility of inviting one parent new to the group. Systematically increasing the number of parents leads to more parental input and enhanced representation of needs. At Stage 2, the core group of parents also has greater responsibility for organizing, leading, and setting dates for additional meetings. Parents from the core group emerge as leaders helping to create a low-risk environment for new participants and leading conversations to identify additional needs.

The Latina mother who secured traffic signage in the previous example cochaired the Stage 2 meetings. At these meetings, the parents new to the group listened to the original core group describe their process for creating change. At each Stage 2 meeting, repeated accounts of what the core group had accomplished demonstrated the possibilities of what could be gained when parents express their needs and wants through an organized process. Moreover, repeated accounts of accomplishments set precedence and procedures for setting future goals.

By Stage 3, the purpose and process for conducting the meetings are well established and familiar to the core group. At this point, parents have gained the knowledge and skills to set their own agenda and lead meetings, recognizing that they can problem-solve through an effective mechanism that allows them to articulate their needs.

Dialogue journals (written exchanges between parents and teachers) are a valuable tool that can be used throughout the three stages. They offer another mode of listening to parents' needs, especially those parents who may be reluctant to speak aloud. Parents can be motivated to participate in dialogue journals when they understand that the purpose is to exchange ideas, ask questions, provide comments, or express concerns about their child's education. Dialogue journals are a clear indication that parents' input is valued, and they can help to establish a trusting partnership between home and school. Dialogue journals, however, must be an optional activity. It is important to consider the perceived risks that some parents may associate with writing and literacy. For example, parents may not have previously enjoyed freedom of expression, their literacy may be incomplete, or their participation may expose a lack of practice in reading and writing. Moreover, parents may have the notion that their native language or their ideas are not valued at school. In addition, some parents will be hesitant about keeping a dialogue journal if they are uncertain of how their thoughts and ideas will be used. For example, parents may be fearful that disagreeing with a school practice or district policy may create problems for their child. We strongly recommend assuring parents that they can freely write in their preferred language, that their ideas are more important than their use of conventional spelling and grammar structure, and that dialogue journals are confidential and shared only with the parents' permission.

Work collaboratively with parents to establish the parameters and procedures associated with journaling. These parameters and procedures should establish a purpose and a range of topics that reflect the interest of all participants. Some points of discussion may include the following:

- How often do we exchange dialogue journals?
- Will we comment on each other's dialogue journal?

- With whom can we share the content of dialogue journals?
- When do we raise the content (wants and needs) in a public forum?
- How do we raise the content of dialogue journals in a public forum?

The purpose for journaling and the topics selected should inspire parents to communicate their needs, ideas, questions, and concerns regarding their child's education, about education in general, or about how their community influences education. You might consider involving students in writing journal entries along with their parents, especially students in grades 3 and above. Figure 2.2 outlines a model for carrying out journaling activities. You can use it as a guide and adapt it to meet the particular issues and needs that are pertinent to the parents you serve.

FIGURE 2.2
Steps for Parent–Teacher Dialogue Journaling

1. State the purposes for journaling, which are the following:
   - To establish communication about their child.
   - To provide parents opportunities to share ideas, questions, and concerns about a topic linked to classroom instruction, education, or the community in general.
2. Explain how often journaling exchanges will occur, which can be negotiated.
3. Explain the expected benefits, which are the following:
   - Parents are the child's first teachers and as such can share best approaches to support the child's learning preferences, interests, and other factors.
   - This information can be integrated with daily instruction to make learning more relevant and interesting.
   - Parents can share knowledge about life in their community, including their social and cultural capital.
4. Explain who will have access to the journal entries. Indicate that journaling should be a confidential and professional activity between the teacher and parents. Discuss where and how the journals will be safeguarded.
5. Reiterate that parents can add their own ideas, questions, needs, and concerns about school and their community.

Parents who have invested time, effort, and energy in the three-stage model have become more familiar and comfortable with the process of voicing their needs and more trusting that the process is in their best interest. In Stage 3, parents will expand their knowledge about legislated policies that affect their lives. It is the teacher's responsibility to research governing entities at various levels that affect children, families, and communities that teachers serve. Figure 2.3 can guide you through the

FIGURE 2.3

Assessing How Policies Align with Voiced Needs

Levels to Consider	Questions to Contemplate	What I Discovered
At the federal level, identify— • Senators • Representatives	• How has past legislation affected this community? • How will forthcoming legislation affect this community? • How closely is legislation aligned with the voiced needs of the community? • Do parents know who these representatives are? • Do parents know what their role is?	
At the state level, identify— • Governor • Senators • Representatives • School board	• How has past legislation affected this community? • How will forthcoming legislation affect this community? • How closely is legislation aligned with the voiced needs of the community? • Do parents know who these representatives are? • Do parents know what their role is?	
At the city level, identify— • Mayor • City council representatives	• How have past ordinances/policies affected this community? • How will forthcoming ordinances/policies affect this community? • How closely are ordinances/policies aligned with the voiced needs of the community? • Do parents know who these representatives are? • Do parents know what their role is?	
At the school governance level, identify— • Superintendent • School board • Principal	• How have past policies affected this community? • How will forthcoming policies affect this community? • How closely are policies aligned with the voiced needs of the community? • Do parents know who these representatives are? • Do parents know what their role is?	
Community leaders	• Can parents identify community leaders (church, school, other)? • Whom do parents consult when they encounter problems within the community?	

process, which includes identifying government representatives at the federal, state, and city levels, as well as school district governance and community leaders, including pastors, community activists, and coalition organizers.

Teacher knowledge about government representatives is useful to parents, who can use this information to solve problems within the community. For example, parents might want to petition the proper authorities to minimize the feral animal population, repair streets, control street drainage, remove graffiti, arrange for pick-up of brush and large items, and so forth. More important, over time parents can gain confidence in advocating for community needs. Parent activism at any level can be a positive force for schools and families across the community.

Ultimately, responsive schooling practices and an ethic of care should inspire teachers to continuously forge formal and informal opportunities to engage parents in their child's education.

TAKE **ACTION**

- Identify differences and commonalities among Latino parents.
- Familiarize parents with schooling standards and expectations.
- Contemplate expectations Latino parents have for their children.
- Take a proactive stance to establish trust and common educational goals.
- Organize meetings with parents to effectively solicit their voiced needs.
- Be an active listener during small, core group meetings to engender familiarity and trust.
- Engage parents through dialogue journaling activities.
- Provide parents with information regarding their government representatives.

3

Partnering with Latino Families: An Asset-Based Approach

The previous chapters have offered information to guide you in understanding your worldview and the Latino culture and in engaging Latino parents through an ethic of care. This chapter provides additional information about the native language and principles of language learning and continues to shift the paradigm from a deficit view of culturally and linguistically diverse children and families to an asset-based approach. Taking an asset-based approach in serving Latino families supports the development of home-to-school partnerships based on meaningful relationships.

Viewing Native Language as an Asset

We know that the native language of young Latino children is nurtured at home by parents and in the community where they live (Pérez, 2004). Learning through the native language generates a knowledge base that serves English language learners in future language-learning experiences, and the native language is a critical attribute that distinguishes English language learners from their monolingual peers. We know, too, that the linguistic environment in which Latino children are raised varies from home to home (Romaine, 2001). Here are some of the ways in which Latino English language learners' linguistic environments may vary:

- Parents or caretakers within the home may speak only Spanish.
- Parents or caretakers may speak only Spanish, but there may be no other Spanish speakers (or only a limited number) within the community.
- Parents or caretakers may be of non-native background but are speakers of Spanish.
- Parents or caretakers within the home may speak two languages.
- Parents or caretakers may speak a regional dialect that is honored because it is the language of the home.

As we noted in Chapter 1, the different ways that Latino children speak Spanish are influenced by cultural background and geography. You can value a student's native language by following these guiding principles:

- *Recognize that language variations emerge from particular speech communities.* Understanding these variations can inform you about how students think about and use language as well as produce oral and written language.
- *Respect the languages that students speak.* Although one style of language production may seem more conventional than another, avoid assigning a higher status to one over another. Children's use of language is linked to their identity and particular speech community.
- *Respond positively through an additive approach.* Remember that you are the language role model for all students and are responsible for teaching academic language. However, to establish a rich language-learning environment, the focus of communication is always student-centered and targeted on meaning and purpose. While honoring varying forms of communication, provide scaffolding for the academic language without disrupting the flow of communication or the intent of the speaker's message.

Consider how the teacher in the following example values the language production of her students:

Student	Nonconventional Language Production	Response That Values Language Production
Lucy: "She be mean."	Conjugation of the verb "to be"	Teacher: "Who is mean, Lucy?"
Raker: "It don't matter."	Third-person plural form used instead of the singular	Teacher: "It doesn't matter, Raker? Why doesn't it matter?"
Roberto: "*No toches eso porque se quiebra.*"	Code mixing for the word "touch" (*tocar* in Spanish)	Teacher: "*Sí, no lo toques porque se quiebra.*" (Yes, do not touch it because it breaks.)

Bilingual children frequently encounter negative attitudes toward unconventional language use at school; they may experience a devaluing of the way they communicate and may receive deficit instructional approaches that stress mimicry, memorization, and repetition. Providing remediation to "fix" errors in language production undermines Latino English language learners' efforts to learn English and casts negative views about the use of their own native language, both of which negatively influence self-esteem and self-efficacy. Consequently, we urge teachers to practice asset-based instructional approaches by viewing children's language production as part of a continuum of development, by valuing the thoughts they communicate, by not interrupting children's expressed ideas through error correction, and by building students' proficiency through the modeling of conventional modes of language use. A well-trained, certified ESL teacher is knowledgeable about how to create appropriate, relevant, and authentic instruction that sustains language development in both the first and second language.

Recognizing Readiness to Learn

From an early age, children know that their parents are their first teachers, and as they grow, parents provide interesting surroundings to explore, which helps children make sense of the world around them. Accordingly, every child has unique experiences, and these frame the child's knowledge of the world (Diaz-Rico, 2004). Whereas some children may have a wide range of educational toys to stimulate their cognitive development and are taken to libraries, zoos, and museums that pique their curiosity, others may have limited access to such resources. Social competence, communicative competence, critical thinking, and problem solving, however, are not defined by socioeconomic status. Whatever the circumstances, the dynamic of the home establishes a foundation for learning that schooling will enhance.

Informal knowledge is also important and can be gained during play at home that involves problem-solving activities, which in turn allow young children to engage in negotiation skills. Playing with peers highlights the importance of learning through social interaction, as emphasized by Vygotsky (Kozulin, 2000). As social interaction expands, young children add to their informal knowledge. Consider the following example of three 5-year-olds playing "store" in their backyard. They have gathered assorted items, including empty food containers, small toys, and sticks that represent items to be sold at their store. They cut up a banana plant leaf into strips to represent dollars and gather smaller leaves from another plant to represent coins. Julieta has assumed the role of storekeeper and assigned the other two children to be the customers. They must agree on what each item represents and how to price each item. A conflict arises over one stick that represents the candy that both customers want to buy. Julieta cannot make a decision, so Josefina and Javier come to an agreement after arguing a bit because both want to continue playing. Josefina tells Javier that she will buy the candy and break it in half. However, Javier must give Josefina two small leaves in exchange. Javier agrees, and the children continue playing store.

In this example, the children demonstrated the following skills that are associated with academic learning:

- *Social competence.* The children perceived and appropriately responded to body language, facial expressions, and gestures (nonverbal communication) throughout the exchanges during play.
- *Communicative competence.* The children engaged in and managed conversations to avoid communication breakdowns. They also considered with whom they were communicating as they negotiated the meaning of the items involved in their play.
- *Critical thinking and problem solving.* The children applied their background knowledge (how a store operates), evaluated the situation (recognized the problem), and problem-solved (broke the stick in two).

Consider the following culture-specific example of play and how it promotes critical thinking (Pellegrini & Galda, 1993). *Lobo, Lobito ¿Estás Ahí?* (Wolf, Little Wolf, Are You There?) is a popular Latino children's game similar to Duck, Duck, Goose with its element of surprise. The object of this game is for the "wolf" to chase and catch its unsuspecting prey (the children). To play the game, one child is chosen to be the wolf. Other children line up a few feet away from the wolf, whose back is turned toward the group. The game starts when the children recite, "*Juguemos en el bosque; lobo, lobito ¿estás ahí?*" (Let's play in the forest; wolf, little wolf, are you there?). To engage the element of surprise, the wolf comes up with excuses to explain why he is not ready to play. He might respond, "I'm putting on my socks." The children repeat the question, and the wolf may say, "I'm putting on my coat." The process continues ("I'm looking for my keys," "I'm slipping on my shoes," "I'm shaving") until the wolf says, "I'm on my way out to eat all of you" and begins to chase the children. The children run to a safe home base, and those that are caught can play wolf in the next round of play. Consider the problem solving that this game elicits when the children have to contemplate what it might take for the wolf to prepare himself for the day and evaluate when to run away and how to avoid being caught. The wolf has to think of many ways to prepare for the day. Children engage in critical thinking when they elaborate their responses: "I'm cleaning my glasses," "I'm making a fresh pot of coffee," "I'm getting my briefcase," and so on. Children learn the rules and object of the game, turn taking, and how to negotiate disagreements that may emerge.

Other academic-related principles are learned at home as well. Think of all the household chores that children can possibly be assigned to do: cooking, preparing meals, baby sitting, vacuuming, window washing, sweeping, taking out the trash, washing clothes, cutting grass, and gardening, for example. In all of these activities, children may be exposed to mathematical and scientific concepts such as decision making, evaluating, measuring, estimating, sorting, and classifying. Many also involve following directions and sequencing steps to effectively complete each task.

Similar principles are at work in routines associated with religious practices. Latinos who are Protestants, for example, will teach their children the religious expressions associated with a particular denomination, including worship practices, Sunday school attendance, and participation in other church-related events. In a Catholic Latino household, the family may display an altar with religious relics. The family may regularly gather around the altar to pray for loved ones. Some families light candles as a sign of perpetual prayer. The parents may ask their children to monitor the candle and remind them to buy a new one when it is spent. In each instance, parents have not only modeled expressions of religious worship; they have also taught important routines and assigned responsibilities that have provided children with informal knowledge that may influence learning at school.

Academic principles can also be directly or indirectly applied and reinforced when children watch television shows, cartoons, and movies with their families and then deliberate over them, and you can connect your lessons to movies and shows that are familiar to your students. An example comes from Mrs. Vargas, a 4th grade teacher who had several recent-immigrant students with limited prior schooling experience in her classroom. To help them understand the organization and the elements of a story, she asked them to share a movie they had watched. When some of the girls commented that they preferred watching *novelas* (soap operas) with their mother or grandmother, Mrs. Vargas asked the girls to describe the following elements: who the actors were, where it took place, what had happened up to specific points, the problems the characters encountered, and how they solved them. In this way, Mrs. Vargas used the information provided by students to introduce the various story elements: characters, setting, sequence of events, conflict, and resolution.

You can also capitalize on students' inquiries and use them to develop higher-order thinking skills. When students talk about their own experiences, you can offer opportunities to extend student thinking about the topic at hand. For example, for a lesson about adjectives, Mrs. Green brought an egg to class and asked her 1st graders to describe it. Students brainstormed words such as "white," "smooth," and "small." One child described the different ways her grandmother has prepared eggs for breakfast. Rather than dismissing the child's comments, the teacher encouraged her to keep a log of the different characteristics she observed as the eggs were being cooked in different ways. The teacher guided this learning experience by helping the student draw important connections across concepts associated with language arts and science (physical changes, observational skills, and so forth).

These various scenarios demonstrate that all children enter school with knowledge that they have acquired at home and through their social networks of parents, siblings, friends, and community members and through media experiences. Indeed, Latino children come to school ready to learn and to enhance their existing knowledge. Valuing students' knowledge, experiences, and interests is beneficial to instruction when you use this knowledge base to enrich classroom learning.

Understanding that Latino children and their families have assets that contribute to their own education is fundamental. In the following sections we offer a range of possible ways to connect Latino parents with schools. To effectively implement these ideas, it is important to reflect on the suggestions and revise them based on the needs of the Latino families in your community.

Creating a Welcoming School Environment

Positive relationships between schools and Latino households can create an environment in which students' families feel they belong. All teachers have a personal responsibility for creating a positive, inclusive school climate for parents that is based on two-way communication. The first step is to assess the existing climate of the entire campus. Determine how accessible the various personnel are at the front office, in the counseling department, in health services, and in the special areas such as art, music, and P.E. Identify how accommodating school personnel are when responding to parent inquiries. For example, school staff members with a limited understanding of Spanish and the Latino culture may unknowingly create social barriers that obstruct effective two-way communication between parents and school personnel. Here are some questions to consider in assessing whether your school has a welcoming environment:

- How well do personnel communicate with parents?
- How friendly are they?
- How do they demonstrate a disposition for accommodating parents?
- How efficient are they in identifying individuals who can facilitate communication?
- How resourceful are they in identifying or providing information parents need?

It is important for all school personnel to become familiar with the community they serve (as we discussed in Chapter 1) and to develop appropriate skills to create a welcoming school environment. It may be advisable for the campus leadership team to identify qualified personnel to work specifically toward the goal of engendering a positive school climate. Together with the leadership team, teachers can begin by establishing a rapport with parents. Even little gestures can have a big impact. For example, school personnel can show that they care about the students and their families by greeting them with a smile when they arrive at or depart from school. A simple "Good morning, *Buenos días*" and "Have a good day, *Que tengan un buen día*" can also make a difference in helping parents feel secure. In their greetings, teachers can share positive messages with parents about their children.

In addition to personal interactions with Latino parents of English language learners, the physical environment reflects the spirit of the school community. Signs, campus activity calendars, other posted information written in the parents' native language, and chairs in the foyer or lobby convey a commitment to maintain an inclusive community. See Figure 3.1 for examples of phrases that school personnel may use or display around the school to make Latino parents feel welcome.

Another aspect of the Latino culture to keep in mind when thinking about how teachers interact with Latino parents of English language learners is the value placed on individuals above institutions—a concept known as *personalismo* (Chong & Baez, 2005). In U.S. school culture, teachers are expected to address all parents in a formal, businesslike manner, but some Latino parents may perceive this communication style to be impersonal. Keep in mind that many Latino parents may prefer to establish friendly rapport on a personal level, with direct communication. To initiate such rapport, you can make phone calls to introduce yourself to parents, and you can use your first contact to invite them to attend Meet the Teacher/Orientation Night or other events at the beginning of the school year. After talking to the parents or caretakers, you may then send a written invitation (Reproducibles A.2a and A.2b in Appendix A provide examples of a letter to inform parents and to request their presence at Meet

FIGURE 3.1
Phrases to Display Around the School

All minds are precious.	*Todas las mentes son preciosas.*
Helping students succeed.	*Ayudando a que triunfen los estudiantes.*
It is a pleasure to work with you and your family.	*Es un placer trabajar con usted y su familia.*
It is great to have you in our school.	*Es un placer tenerlo(s) en nuestra escuela.*
Let's work together for our children.	*Trabajemos juntos por nuestros niños.*
Our children's work.	*El trabajo de nuestros niños.*
Parents and teachers are partners in their children's education.	*Los padres y maestros son socios en la educación de los niños.*
Teachers and parents working together.	*Padres y maestros trabajando juntos.*
Thank you for being here.	*Gracias por estar aquí.*
Thank you for investing your time and talents in your children's education.	*Gracias por invertir su tiempo y talentos en la educación de sus hijos.*
Together we learn.	*Juntos aprendemos.*
We appreciate our families.	*Apreciamos a nuestras familias.*
We are a good team.	*Somos un buen equipo.*
We are happy that you are part of our community.	*Estamos contentos de que sea(n) parte de nuestra comunidad.*
We are not complete without you.	*No estamos completos sin usted(es).*
We enjoy working with you.	*Disfrutamos trabajar con usted(es).*
Welcome.	*Bienvenido(s).*
You make the difference in this school.	*Usted(es) hace(n) la diferencia en esta escuela.*
Your family is important to us.	*Su familia es importante para nosotros.*

the Teacher/Orientation Night). Figure 3.2 provides Spanish translations for common phrases that can be used to introduce parents to school personnel.

In their attempt to get to know their children's teacher, some Latino parents may ask questions that some may perceive as being too personal. For example, when parents want to know more about your background they may ask, "Do you have a family of your own?" "Do you have a boyfriend?" or "How many children do you have?" With the premise of *personalismo* in mind, respond to their interest but offer only information that you are comfortable sharing. Here are some ways to provide information about your background:

- Develop a "This Is Me" poster or bulletin board to display outside or inside the classroom. It can include pictures of family, a list of schools attended, activities you enjoy, and other artifacts. The display can include text in both Spanish and English.
- Plan a "Spotlight on the Teacher" day when students' families are invited to come and hear you share experiences from your previous teaching or tell them about a special talent you have and can share.
- Arrange to have lunch or dinner with each of your student's families so they can get to know you outside the classroom and you can get to know them.

FIGURE 3.2
Phrases of Introduction in Spanish

Nice to meet you.	*Mucho gusto.*
I am your son's/daughter's teacher.	*Yo soy la maestra/el maestro de su hijo(a).*
Let me introduce you to....	*Permítame presentarle a....*
He/she is the principal.	*El/ella es el/la director(a).*
He/she is the counselor.	*El/ella es el/la consejero(a).*
He/she works in the office.	*El/ella trabaja en la oficina.*
He/she works with your child.	*El/ella trabaja con su niño(a).*
These are the school rules.	*Estas son las reglas de la escuela.*
These are our classroom rules.	*Estas son las reglas de nuestro salón.*
This is our homework procedure.	*Este es nuestro procedimiento de tarea.*
This is our attendance procedure.	*Este es nuestro procedimiento de asistencia.*

Teachers have many opportunities to interact with Latino parents formally and informally. These include a variety of scheduled school events such as PTA (PTO) meetings, parent–teacher meetings, and carnivals and other special occasions. Consider how Mrs. Nunley, a 1st grade teacher, started a conversation with the parent of one of her students at a school carnival and was surprised that the parent asked many questions about her child's progress. Perhaps the informal nature of the gathering helped build trust and confidence. In any case, the teacher's willingness to spend time with the parent demonstrated a genuine interest in the child. This scenario highlights the importance of taking the time to show parents that teachers care about their students as individuals. Dedicating time to interact with parents can nurture relationship building and promote ongoing communication.

Also, it is common for many Latino parents to invite their child's teachers to family celebrations, such as *quinceañeras*, weddings, and baptisms. In a different community, Mr. Pitt, a 1st grade teacher, attended the birthday party of one of his students and enjoyed meeting the child's relatives. The informal nature of the gathering made it easy for different family members to ask questions they would not likely have asked in the school setting. Mr. Pitt's attendance and active participation at the family event communicated an interest in his student's life and fostered positive relationships between the parents and the school.

Guiding Parents to Become Partners

Keep in mind that parents and teachers may perceive parental engagement differently. Although parents and teachers share the responsibility of sustaining a home-to-school partnership, the responsibility of making parents feel welcome and secure during each visit belongs to teachers and other school personnel. Schools hold the institutional authority to operate school systems, which parents must learn to navigate. As you think about creating opportunities for parent–teacher collaboration, consider the following questions:

- How well do the Latino parents in your school know how the U.S. education system operates?
- How well do the Latino parents know how your school operates?

As we noted earlier, parents from a middle-class background have experiences and expectations that are largely aligned with school expectations, and this alignment facilitates their children's integration into the school system. In contrast, Latino parents of English language learners may have different schooling backgrounds, their experiences may be mismatched with the expectations of schooling in the United States, and they may need to be informed about particular practices. Here are examples of school practices that are common to students from the mainstream culture:

- Attending school for the full day starting in kindergarten or 1st grade
- Going on field trips and knowing that some may require a fee
- Accessing technology at school and at home
- Participating in after-school programs at the school campus
- Seeing a school nurse when ill and being referred to seek extended medical care if needed
- Consulting a school counselor when there is a problem
- Participating in school fund-raising activities, among other school-related activities

A Latino parent's background knowledge may not include some or all of these activities, but that does not define the parent's capability or potential for fully participating in such activities, which are part of the educational experience in the United States.

Unfamiliarity with school routines and protocols, and feeling unprepared to fulfill what schools require, may cause some Latino parents to perceive that expectations about schooling are insurmountable. Coordinating campus tours for parents can alleviate their feelings of being overwhelmed, and brief seminars can help explain the role of schools, how expectations are aligned with state and national standards, how parents are key partners in the home-to-school connection, and how relationships between home and school are vital to the academic achievement of their child.

Using Technology to Communicate

Technology is a wonderful tool for teachers. Personal computers, cell phones, and many other electronic devices create opportunities for collaboration with parents and communication with students outside of class, and the Internet has become an important way to stay connected. In fact, most districts and their schools have websites that allow teachers to design their own web page. You can use these to post general information about your classroom, including a philosophy statement, classroom management plan, and homework policy. Additionally, you may consider creating links to a calendar of events, a personal biography, the class schedule, daily assignments, student expectations, classroom rules, class news, a picture gallery of class events (be sure to check the district policy on using pictures of students), an FAQ section, and contact information.

To foster a collaborative relationship with Latino parents, you can give your contact information to students' families. Many parents find it important to have the school's telephone number handy in case they have questions or need to leave a message for their child's teacher. You can also encourage communication through e-mail, as some Latino parents have easy access to e-mail and may prefer to contact school personnel electronically. Nowadays, it is standard practice to post all contact information on the school's website, which gives parents several ways to communicate with school personnel. One kindergarten teacher we know distributes business cards she makes on her personal computer, including all of her contact information.

You can also add a blog to your individual web pages. Informational items that are posted and displayed on a blog provide opportunities for ongoing communication between teachers, parents, and students. According to Davis (2004), classroom blogs may also be used to describe a specific teaching unit, build a class newsletter, post prompts for writing, provide examples of class assignments, display spelling words, upload photos of class activities, and showcase students' work. Moreover, when parents read their children's classroom blog, they can provide comments and suggestions about the learning that is occurring. Students and parents can also contribute to these blogs by adding information about educational activities they do together. After learning that his son was studying animal adaptations in his class, for instance, one father posted information about his family's recent visit to the zoo. Together, the father and son wrote an essay explaining that what the child learned at school helped them better understand the habitats of the captive animals. Another teacher who asks her students to take home the classroom hamster over the weekend also invites them to contribute to the class blog detailing everything they did to care for it—a good example of using technology in creative ways while encouraging students to apply academic skills.

Most teachers already know about the existence of seemingly endless websites devoted to the education of children. Because many Latino parents do not have an education background and the training in child development that teachers do, many do not know how to distinguish a sound website from an unreliable one. Thus, consider sending parents the addresses of websites that are a valid resource and are endorsed by education experts. Figure 3.3 is a list of useful websites, and Reproducibles A.3a and A.3b in Appendix A are letters in English and Spanish, respectively, that you can send parents informing them of websites that you find beneficial.

With your help, the campus leadership team can designate a computer area for parents. Parents who do not have access to technology at home thus can be encouraged to use available school computers to access the information they may need. In addition, by using technology, parents gain valuable skills they can later apply to working with their children. Consider the following scenario, which illustrates how schools can create opportunities for parents to interact with their children and learn together.

FIGURE 3.3
Useful Websites

http://www.colorincolorado.org

This bilingual website includes resources for families of English language learners and for the professionals (e.g., teachers, librarians) who work with them. Information about where to find culturally and linguistically relevant literature, as well as research about working with English learners, is provided.

http://www.learningpage.com

This site offers teaching resources that can be incorporated into lesson plans, including a gallery of printable materials teachers can use to reinforce a variety of concepts.

http://www.primarygames.com

Games and activities that can be used to supplement the curriculum across content areas are available at this website.

http://www.raz-kids.com

This reading library allows the students to listen to stories, read for practice, record their own reading, and answer comprehension questions about passages they have read.

http://www.readinga-z.com

This is an online reading resource center that provides books at varying reading levels. Information about the kinds of books (e.g., multilevel, wordless, high-frequency word books) is also provided, as well as ideas for incorporating phonics, fluency, and vocabulary teaching into lessons.

http://www.readingrockets.org

In addition to resources about teaching reading, this bilingual website provides specific classroom strategies to use when working with struggling readers in the areas of print awareness, phonological awareness, phonics, fluency, vocabulary, and comprehension. A description of each strategy is provided, as well as information about when to use it (e.g., before, during, or after reading).

http://www.schoolexpress.com

This website contains thematic units, worksheets, and free reading books for teachers to access. It also provides links to electronic workbooks for all content areas and educational websites.

http://www.sciencea-z.com

Instructional units are available within four categories: life science, physical science, earth science, and process science.

http://www.softschools.com

This website provides a variety of worksheets, games, and activities that can be used as homework or to supplement specific lessons, organized by grades and topics. Resources are also available in Spanish and French.

http://www.vocabularya-z.com

The website enables teachers to create individualized lessons to improve their students' vocabulary. Activities, games, and graphic organizers for increasing vocabulary are available.

http://www.writinga-z.com

Lessons and tools to teach the writing process are available, along with ideas for how to organize and improve student writing.

An elementary school enlisted the help of local college students to provide additional reading instruction to the children. The school's leadership team designated a classroom for the tutoring (they called it the "Hall of Great Readers") where the college students individually tutored struggling readers. Most of the youngsters received about two hours of tutoring a week. Parents were invited to sit through the tutoring sessions and learn the specific reading strategies the college students were using. In one instance, a parent noticed that the tutor used a game in which the child had to identify letter names and sounds. When the parent asked where she could learn similar strategies, the tutor took her to the computer and showed her the websites where strategies were available. Together, they identified websites that the child could use to improve his reading performance. In time, the mother became more familiar with the Internet and was able to share her new knowledge with her children and other parents.

Conducting Home Visits

Conducting home visits is another way in which teachers—together with the campus leadership team—can develop partnerships with Latino families. In addition to gaining insight about children's lives outside of school, teachers who visit students' homes may discover additional social barriers that exist between home and school. Consider the following scenario.

Eva was a student in Mr. Garza's bilingual kindergarten classroom. At the beginning of the school year, Mr. Garza wanted to increase Eva's parents' involvement at school and used typical modes of written communication, such as newsletters, notes, and letters. However, Eva's parents did not respond. Mr. Garza wondered if her parents had received his notes requesting conferences to discuss Eva's academic progress. He had only met Eva's parents during registration. At that time they did not ask questions and left school quickly after completing the enrollment process. As the school year progressed, Eva's parents did not show up for parent–teacher conferences and did not attend any other school functions. Because Eva rode the bus to school, Mr. Garza surmised that he could not see Eva's parents after school. He also was unsuccessful in his attempts to reach them by phone. After thinking about ways to communicate with Eva's family because he wanted to talk with them about how to help Eva succeed in school, he decided to make a home visit.

Mr. Garza was proactive in attempting to engage Eva's parents. During his home visit, he found out that the parents' English proficiency was limited and they couldn't decipher the various communications sent home. Eva's parents shared that they had recently immigrated to the United States to give their daughter a better education. Like their daughter, both attended ESL classes and were advancing their knowledge. They attempted to read and to make sense of the written information that was sent home, but their comprehension was limited. Mr. Garza explained the differences between informational correspondence and forms that required a signature. Together, Mr. Garza and Eva's parents developed a plan for the family to return important paperwork. Their solution was to color-code the various kinds of school correspondence. Mr. Garza would use green paper to photocopy informational paperwork, and any correspondence that had to be returned would be copied on blue paper. This strategy enabled Eva's parents to distinguish the correspondence, and if they had any questions they could call Mr. Garza. In extending a symbolic hand in partnership, Mr. Garza succeeded in keeping Eva's parents informed about their daughter's education.

Although this example shows how home visits can provide unanticipated benefits for everyone involved, such visits are not a component of the traditional model for enhancing parental engagement by schools. Guidelines for when and how to conduct them may be unclear or in some cases nonexistent at the school or district level. Figure 3.4 outlines some guidelines, and Figure 3.5 includes conversation starters you can use. (See Reproducible A.4 in Appendix A for a form for documenting observations and what transpired during the visit.)

Translating School Documents and Information

Teachers of English language learners who value their students' native language provide written communication to parents in that language as a way of increasing their participation at school. The letters, notes, and other school documents that are written in English should be written with the same degree of professionalism in Spanish. If you do not speak Spanish, you can identify colleagues to serve as resources to meet this objective. Colleagues or school volunteers who are proficient speakers of Spanish and who possess strong literacy skills represent potential linguistic brokers. Not only can they bridge and sustain communication between teachers and Latino parents, they can also translate documents and serve as interpreters or school liaisons.

Consider the example of Mrs. Salinas and her contributions to her child's school. Mrs. Salinas, a former musician and guitarist in her native Mexico, volunteered in her child's music class for an entire school year. The music teacher, Mrs. Archer, asked her principal to consider Mrs. Salinas as a resource person who could translate school documents. Although Mrs. Salinas had a strong musical background, it was her command of Spanish literacy and her developing acquisition of English that made her the obvious candidate to meet this critical need. The principal recognized these assets and asked Mrs. Salinas to shift from volunteering in the music class to translating school documents.

FIGURE 3.4
Guidelines for Home Visits

Before your visit…

- Notify the parent of your upcoming home visit if possible. If you have not been able to reach parents via letter or phone, ask the child to let the parents know when you will be visiting their home and the reasons for that visit.
- Review the child's records and learn about his or her cultural background and family history. Ask about the child's family members (who the child lives with at home) and try to learn their names.
- Have a plan for each visit. Set an amount of time for each home visit (45 to 60 minutes), but try to be flexible with how that time is used. Be aware that during the first visits, you may need to spend time getting to know people in the household and giving them the opportunity to get to know you.
- Make sure you leave a schedule of home visits with your school secretary or administrator.

During your visit…

- Introduce yourself and engage parents and family members in small talk. This helps to establish a social connection and begins to develop a relationship of trust.
- Explain the purpose of your visit (e.g., to learn about the family, to discuss the child's academic progress) and elicit parent feedback regarding other kinds of information they would like to discuss with you.
- Be ready to share academic information regarding the child, as well as information about other resources families may need for special issues or circumstances (e.g., medical assistance for an ill relative, where and how to get help for a young child with a disability).
- Observe the family and the interactions between the child and caregiver. Use your visit as an opportunity to learn from your student and to model teaching opportunities with parents.

After your visit…

- Document the visit (see Reproducible A.4 in Appendix A).
- Reflect on what you learned.
- Think about ways to incorporate the information parents shared with you and other information you gathered from your home visit into your teaching.

Latino parents appreciate the efforts school personnel take in translating school documents and notices into their native language. Frequently, individuals who translate school documents also become interpreters for Latino parents. At one elementary school, Mrs. Castro, a bilingual teaching assistant, had been invited to accompany several parents when they met with their child's teacher, who spoke only English. At the meeting, Mrs. Castro interpreted for Mrs. Aguilar because the parent did not

FIGURE 3.5
Conversation Starters for Home Visits

Good morning/good afternoon/good evening.	*Buenos días/buenas tardes/buenas noches.*
How are you/your family?	*¿Cómo está usted/su familia?*
Thank you for welcoming me into your home.	*Gracias por abrirme las puertas de su casa.*
I am honored to be here.	*Es un honor estar aquí.*
Who lives with you at the house?	*¿Quiénes viven con usted?*
How long have you lived here?	*¿Cuánto tiempo tienen viviendo aquí?*
Where did you live before?	*¿Dónde vivía antes?*
I am glad you are now part of our community.	*Me da gusto que ahora sea parte de nuestra comunidad.*
Let me tell you what we are learning in school.	*Déjeme decirle lo que estamos aprendiendo en la escuela.*
Let me tell you why what we are doing in school is important.	*Déjeme decirle por qué es importante lo que estamos haciendo en la escuela.*
Let me tell you how you can help your child at home.	*Déjeme decirle cómo puede ayudarle a su hijo(a) en casa.*
Have you received letters from the school or from your child's teacher?	*¿Ha recibido cartas de la escuela o del/de la maestro (a) de su hijo(a)?*
What do you think about the letters and documents you have received?	*¿Qué piensa de las cartas y documentos que ha recibido?*
What questions do you have about these documents?	*¿Qué preguntas tiene acerca de estos documentos?*
Let me tell you why these documents are important.	*Déjeme decirle por qué son importantes estos documentos.*
It is very helpful when you return these documents to school.	*Nos ayuda mucho cuando usted regresa estos documentos a la escuela.*
Together we can make the best decisions for your child's education.	*Juntos podemos tomar las mejores decisiones para la educación de su hijo(a).*
What questions do you have for me?	*¿Qué preguntas tiene para mí?*

understand the information that the teacher shared. This would not have been possible had Mrs. Aguilar not developed a trusting relationship with Mrs. Castro at the school. This example demonstrates one way that schools can make use of their existing resources to help Latino parents become valued participating members of the school community.

In some instances—counseling matters, discipline issues, and meetings to assess language proficiency, as well as matters associated with special education, for example—parents with limited English proficiency must assimilate large amounts of information in a short time. These meetings involve issues of equity because the outcomes can significantly affect students and their families; therefore, it is critical that persons fluent in both Spanish and English serve as interpreters. For example, consider the meeting of a school's Individualized Education Plan committee to determine whether a child is eligible for special education services. It can be overwhelming for Latino parents to simultaneously listen to what the school professionals have to say, answer their exhaustive list of questions, interpret the results of psychological and achievement tests, ask questions, and make decisions that will have life-altering effects. A certified bilingual education teacher or a teacher who has a superior command of Spanish and is knowledgeable about the special education process and terminology could be identified to serve as a qualified interpreter. Parents can also benefit from having time after the meeting to review the information or ask questions about the process.

Issues of equity are embedded in all types of school policies and practices. Inequities emerge when responsible school personnel overlook or disregard the importance of communicating effectively with parents who speak a language other than English. In addition, teachers may encounter challenges in meeting their communication objectives when a Latino parent has limited literacy skills in the native language. Providing parents with a recording of written notices, minutes of meetings, and other written material in the native language demonstrates the school's willingness to accommodate Latino parents and their varying needs.

TAKE **ACTION**

- Think about the various assets that your students and their families have.
- Greet children and their families warmly at every opportunity.
- Identify key school personnel to serve as interpreters and translators for parents.
- Give parents a tour and offer a brief orientation, including your school's mission.
- Orient parents to school routines and protocols.
- Inform parents that there are opportunities at home that nurture critical thinking and support academic skills.
- Explain to parents how instruction is aligned with state and national standards.
- Share information about yourself with your students and their families to build trust.
- Provide opportunities for students to use their native language during instruction—for example, peer conferencing, buddy reading, literature circles, or working to solve math problems with a partner.
- Encourage students to lead familiar games, as this creates opportunities to develop leadership, organizational, and decision-making skills.
- Be open to home visits and accepting invitations to family events, which offer opportunities to learn about your students' lives outside of school.

4

Using Multiple Sources to Gather Information

Research has confirmed the crucial role that the native language holds in learning and acquiring a second language (Lindholm-Leary & Borsato, 2006). Therefore, gaining as much information as possible about the linguistic repertoire of each English learner enrolled at your school can inform instructional practices that support language development. In addition, it can improve school intake procedures and support decisions regarding appropriate student placement in programs and classrooms. Parents can provide background information about the language use of their child along with other pertinent information that presents a more comprehensive understanding of a student's knowledge and skills. You can gather such information from parents through structured meetings, by administering formal protocols, and also through friendly and casual conversations, all of which we discuss in this chapter.

Formal Identification and Evaluation of English Language Learners

Many states provide formal protocols that guide schools in identifying and evaluating each language that an English learner may speak. As a term of the Civil Rights Act of 1964, Title VI, Language Minority Compliance Procedures, your school or a designated school district department initially identifies students when parents enroll their child in school. Parents of children who are speakers of languages other than English fill out a questionnaire about the language or languages spoken at home. Some state education departments have named this questionnaire the Home Language Survey. (Reproducibles A.5a and A.5b in Appendix A are English and Spanish versions of such a survey; they may help you locate the specific form your district uses to document students' language proficiency and also help you become familiar with the kind of information you should solicit from parents.) The questions ask parents how different settings and purposes influence their child's use of each language. Clearly, this questionnaire seeks to determine the student's primary language so that children who need instruction in their native language are provided an appropriate program that best meets their developing language needs.

In most states, public schools serving English language learners form a committee that is charged with making decisions about student placements. In Texas, for instance, this committee is called the Language Proficiency Assessment Committee, and in New Mexico, it is called the Language Assessment Committee. The committee or team can include the classroom bilingual education/ESL teacher (certified language support teacher), an administrator, and a parent representative knowledgeable about the native language and the school programs that best serve English language learners. If the student was previously enrolled in a special education program, then the special education teacher is also part of this decision-making team. The committee members are thoroughly trained on the purpose and procedures associated with serving on the committee. They use the Home Language Survey and other pertinent academic information to make decisions about each student's appropriate placement. Additional information may consist of a state-approved assessment to measure the proficiency levels for each language that the child speaks. The language assessment may determine only oral proficiency in both Spanish and English for young children, and other assessments may measure reading and writing in both languages for children in grades 3 and above.

After reaching a decision about the best placement for each English learner, the committee must schedule a meeting with individual parents to explain the evaluation process, to share their recommendations based on data the committee used, to provide thorough information, to discuss expected outcomes of each instructional program they recommend, and to answer questions. Parents, as a key partner, are always encouraged to share information about their child at this meeting. A good way to start the meeting might be to ask questions such as these:

- What would you like to tell us about your child? (*¿Qué le gustaría decirnos acerca de su hijo(a)?*)

- What are your child's strengths, interests, preferences, aspirations, and aversions? (*¿Cuáles son las destrezas, intereses, preferencias, aspiraciones, y aversiones de su hijo(a)?*)
- What are some expectations that you have of us, the classroom teacher, and the school? (*¿Cuáles son algunas de las expectativas que usted tiene de nosotros, del maestro(a), y de la escuela?*)

Consider sharing these questions with parents in advance so that they have time to contemplate their responses. Imagine the advantage of learning from a parent that his 1st grader already reads and writes in Spanish or that her 2nd grader is extremely shy around English speakers and avoids speaking English. The added value that the committee offers is that the classroom teacher can directly benefit from the information gathered from meeting with parents. Teachers can use language assessment results and any information that parents share to prepare instruction aligned with each student's academic needs, developing language needs, and interests. The information can also broaden a teacher's assessment of each student's linguistic and academic progress.

Before a child can be placed in a bilingual education or an ESL classroom, each parent must provide a signed consent form. In fact, parents have the right to deny their child the placement recommended by the committee. This underscores the importance of communicating precise and comprehensive information to parents about the goals and expected outcomes of each program option presented.

Identifying Attitudes Toward Parental Involvement

As just described, the placement meeting is extremely important, and it relies on parents providing complete and accurate information about their children. Obviously, this, in turn, depends to a large extent on the level of trust and comfort that parents feel when they come to the school. Although we have discussed the importance of parents feeling welcome in previous chapters, the topic bears repeating here. Latino parents of English language learners may be reluctant to become involved with school professionals if they sense that they are not welcomed. School staff who have a limited understanding of Spanish and the culture of Latino families may unknowingly create social barriers. Latino parents encounter these barriers when they repeatedly experience difficulty in communicating with school personnel who do not speak Spanish. Because office personnel usually create the school's first public impressions, it is important that the campus leadership team ensure that office staff develop adequate communication skills or that qualified personnel are hired to facilitate communication with parents. As we discussed in Chapter 3, a warm, caring, and welcoming environment for Latino parents of English language learners is one where they can find people who communicate with them in their own language. Even when school personnel do not speak the parents' language, an open-door policy demonstrates a willingness to create a school environment where everyone is invited to come in and share his or her expertise.

Other potential social barriers include negative attitudes toward culturally and linguistically diverse families who may also come from low-income backgrounds. These attitudes may extend to perceptions about parental involvement. The campus leadership team can use Figure 4.1 with their teachers as a starting point to define parental involvement and thereby identify the attitudes—perceptions and misperceptions—that teachers may have. In rating the activities, the teachers can begin to understand how they perceive parents' roles in children's schooling. More important, they can explore the discrepancies that exist between their perceptions and those of the parents. This information will enable the campus leadership team to identify beliefs, gaps, misinformation, and differences in perspectives, among other findings. Teachers and the leadership team can then use the information to address and reconcile differences in perceptions and beliefs by structuring professional development around relevant issues, with the goal of developing advocacy for Latino parental involvement. Keep in mind that advocates of Latino parental involvement—

- Value the human, social, and cultural capital represented in the community.
- Believe that parents instill lifelong learning dispositions in their children that cultivate academic success and potential economic stability.
- Extend equity and access to educational opportunities to all students.
- Respect the values, aspirations, and expectations of the community regarding schooling, which are reflected in the school mission to advance the academic achievement of English language learners.
- Honor the home-to-school connection by providing a rigorous curriculum that integrates the human, social, and cultural capital represented in the community.
- Address the authentic needs of students.
- Inform parents and engage them in genuine decision-making activities.
- Align the daily operations of the campus with the voiced needs of parents, students, and the community.

The campus leadership team can use the discussions that emerge from the survey to outline the expectations the team seeks to communicate to parents, as well as to determine any additional barriers to parental involvement. The team can then structure a campaign to increase parents' participation at school. The same survey can be used with parents to ascertain how they perceive parental involvement. Figure 4.2, which lists specific questions, is another alternative.

FIGURE 4.1

How Do I Define Parental Involvement?

Rate how the activities listed below define parental involvement, circling the numbers and using the following scale: 1 = not very important, 2 = moderately important, 3 = very important. Then, in the space before each category, rank them in order of importance, using 1 for most important, then 2, and so on.

____ Attending PTA (PTO) meetings	1	2	3
____ Attending parent–teacher conferences	1	2	3
____ Ensuring children are healthy	1	2	3
____ Ensuring children are rested	1	2	3
____ Ensuring children have school supplies	1	2	3
____ Ensuring children do their homework	1	2	3
____ Preparing decorations for bulletin boards	1	2	3
____ Sewing outfits for grade-level play	1	2	3
____ Serving as an officer of the PTA (PTO)	1	2	3
____ Serving as a decision maker on campus policy	1	2	3
____ Reading to children in the classroom	1	2	3
____ Shelving library books	1	2	3
____ Posing questions about problems on campus that affect English language learners	1	2	3
____ Maintaining the home language	1	2	3
____ Collaborating to solve problems or make decisions on campus issues	1	2	3
____ Sharing perspectives on education	1	2	3

Being a Welcoming Teacher

Once a child is assigned to a classroom or program, the responsibility for developing a welcoming environment for parents takes on even greater significance for the individual teacher. You can start the partnership process in a number of ways. You can send a note home with the student written in English (some parents or legal guardians may have literacy skills in English) and in Spanish. The note should be affirming, lighthearted, and optimistic, and should convey to parents sentiments like these:

- Welcome. (*Bienvenido.*)
- We are here to help you and your child. (*Estamos aqui para ayudarlo(a) a usted y a su hijo(a).*)
- Please come by. (*Por favor venga.*)
- I want to work with you. (*Quiero trabajar con usted.*)
- Children flourish when parents and teachers work together. (*Los niños se benefician cuando los padres y maestros trabajan juntos.*)
- How should I contact you? (*¿Como puedo hacer para ponerme en contacto con usted?*)

FIGURE 4.2
Questions to Ask Parents to Clarify How They Perceive Parental Involvement

What academic (school) goals do you have for your child?	*¿Cuáles son sus metas escolares para su niño(a)?*
How do you support your child's school achievement?	*¿Cómo apoya los logros escolares de su hijo(a)?*
Do you have daily routines for your child? What are these routines? Why do you maintain these routines?	*¿Mantiene ciertas rutinas cotidianas para su niño(a)?* *¿Cuáles son?* *¿Por qué las mantiene?*
Name some of your child's school achievements.	*Describa algunos logros escolares de su hijo(a).*
Name some of your child's accomplishments at home.	*Describa algunos logros de su niño(a) en el hogar o en la vida familiar.*
What opportunities do you have to participate in school activities?	*Describa las oportunidades que tenga para colaborar o cooperar con actividades escolares.*
Describe any invitations you have received about participating in school activities.	*Describa algunas invitaciones que ha recibido para participar en actividades escolares.*
Describe school activities in which you have participated.	*Describa las actividades escolares en las que ha participado.*
What may prevent you from participating regularly?	*¿Qué le impide participar más frecuentemente?*
Do you know anyone who participates regularly in school activities?	*¿Tiene conocidos que participan con frecuencia en actividades escolares?*

- We want your child to succeed. (*Queremos que su niño(a) tenga éxito.*)
- We want you to be a part of our school community. (*Queremos que usted sea parte de nuestra comunidad escolar.*)
- You are a teacher, too. (*Usted también es maestro(a).*)
- I cannot wait to meet you. (*No puedo esperar a conocerlo(a).*)
- A Spanish-speaking interpreter is available. (*Hay un(a) intèrprete que habla español.*)
- Here is how you can reach me. (*Así puede comunicarse conmigo.*)
- Contact me when you need to. (*Póngase en contacto conmigo cuando necesite.*)

You'll recall that Figure 3.2 in Chapter 3 offers additional affirming sentiments in Spanish, and Reproducibles A.2a and A.2b in Appendix A are sample introductory letters (in English and Spanish) that welcome parents into the school community and invite them to meet with you. You can use these as models for a letter to send home with the children. In your letter, feel free to include some questions that you expect to discuss with the parent on the day of the meeting. (Figure 4.3 lists a wide range of questions that you can ask parents for the purpose of guiding your instruction, clarifying important matters, and gaining insight into parents' goals.) If you do not receive a response, it is worth exploring whether the parents have literacy skills in their native language. In such cases, a casual exchange with them in the schoolyard may spark their interest.

Sending general communications like the introductory letter casts a wide net and may generate a cohort of enthusiastic parents who were just waiting for an invitation to become involved. This group may respond to your questions in writing, they may want to respond through casual conversations in the school hallway before class starts, or they may prefer to contemplate your note until the meeting. In any case, remain receptive, flexible, and sensitive to parents' varying styles of communication.

Soliciting Information at Parent–Teacher Meetings

The parent–teacher meetings that you conduct will vary—some may be brief and casual, others will be more formal and scheduled—and they may have different goals. But the underlying goal is always to engender continuous dialogue with parents about their children. By design, these meetings should provide you with specific background information about individual students.

FIGURE 4.3

Questions to Ask Parents to Guide Instruction

Listening	***Escuchar***
Does your child prefer to listen to the radio or music in Spanish or English?	*¿Prefiere su hijo(a) escuchar la radio o música en español o en inglés?*
Does your child prefer to watch TV in Spanish or English?	*¿Prefiere su hijo(a) ver la televisión en español o en inglés?*
Speaking	***Hablar***
What language does your child speak the most at home?	*¿En qué lenguaje habla más su niño(a) en la casa?*
What language or languages does your child speak during play?	*¿En qué lenguaje o lenguajes habla su hijo(a) mientras juega?*
What language does your child use most when speaking with adults?	*¿Qué lenguaje usa más su hijo(a) cuando habla con adultos?*
What language does your child use most with siblings?	*¿Qué lenguaje usa más su niño(a) con sus hermanos(a)?*
What language does your child use most with friends?	*¿Qué lenguaje usa más su hijo(a) con sus amigos(as)?*
Does your child favor one language over the other?	*¿Prefiere su niño(a) un lenguaje más que el otro?*
Do you have any concerns about your child's speech?	*¿Tiene usted alguna preocupación acerca del habla de su hijo(a)?*
Reading	***Leer***
Describe any activities that involve literacy.	*Describa actividades de lectura y escritura en las que usted se involucre.*
In what language does your child read the most (or is read to)?	*¿En qué lenguaje lee (o se le lee) más (a) su hijo(a)?*
Describe your child's reading ability.	*Describa la habilidad de lectura de su hijo(a).*
What kinds of books does your child like to read?	*¿Qué tipos de libros le gusta leer a su niño(a)?*
What kinds of stories does your child like to read?	*¿Qué tipos de historias le gusta leer a su hijo(a)?*
When do you read to or with your child?	*¿Cuándo lee usted a su niño(a) o con él/ella?*
Do you have any concerns about your child's reading ability?	*¿Tiene alguna preocupación en cuanto a la habilidad de lectura de su hijo(a)?*
Are there some stories from your culture that you would like me to use?	*¿Hay algunas historias de su cultura que le gustaría que yo usara?*
Are there some sayings, nursery rhymes, fairy tales, and folklore that you would like me to include in specific lessons?	*¿Hay algunos dichos, rimas, cuentos, o folclor que le gustaría que yo incluyera en alguna lección en particular?*
Would you be able to read to our class from time to time?	*¿Estaría usted disponible para venir a leer a nuestra clase de vez en cuando?*

FIGURE 4.3
Questions to Ask Parents to Guide Instruction—(*continued*)

Writing	***Escribir***
In what language does your child write the most?	*¿En qué lenguaje escribe más su hijo(a)?*
Do you have any concerns about your child's writing ability?	*¿Tiene alguna preocupación en cuanto a la habilidad de escritura de su niño(a)?*
Describe your child's writing ability.	*Describa la habilidad de escritura de su hijo(a)?*
Interests	***Intereses***
What does your child play with most often?	*¿Con qué juega más su hijo(a)?*
What does your child like to do for fun?	*¿Qué le gusta hacer a él/ella para divertirse?*
What are your child's abilities?	*¿Cuáles son las habilidades de su niño(a)?*
What abilities would you like to see your child strengthen?	*¿Qué habilidades le gustaría ver que su hijo(a) mejorara?*
What are your child's interests?	*¿Cuáles son los intereses de su niño(a)?*
Are most of your child's friends Spanish or English speakers?	*La mayoría de los amigos de su hijo(a), ¿hablan inglés o español?*
School	***Escuela***
What are your child's aspirations?	*¿Cuáles son las aspiraciones de su hijo(a)?*
What are your aspirations for your child?	*¿Cuáles son las aspiraciones que tiene usted para su niño(a)?*
Do you share/talk about these aspirations with your child?	*¿Habla o comparte usted estas aspiraciones con su hijo(a)?*
What are some specific academic or social skills that you want your child to learn by the end of the school year?	*¿Cuáles son algunas áreas académicas o destrezas sociales específicas que le gustaría que aprendiera su hijo(a) para el final del año?*
What are some specific values that you would like me to teach or reinforce?	*¿Cuáles son algunos valores específicos que le gustaría que yo enseñara o reforzara?*
What are some elements from your culture that you would like me to reinforce?	*¿Cuáles son algunos elementos de su cultura que le gustaría que yo reforzara?*
How do you help your child with homework?	*¿Cómo le ayuda usted a su hijo(a) con la tarea?*
What are your child's strengths?	*¿Cuáles son las áreas fuertes o destrezas de su niño(a)?*
What are your child's weaknesses?	*¿Cuáles son las áreas débiles o dificultades de su hijo(a)?*

An initial formal meeting is critical in developing a relationship with each parent. To prepare for and facilitate this first meeting, think about previous encounters and observations to identify any specific needs parents may have. More specifically, consider the following:

- What is the parent's work schedule? Consider time constraints and plan for meetings to accommodate parents.
- What language is the parent more comfortable speaking? An interpreter may be needed to facilitate the meeting. Ask parents if they want an interpreter.
- Will child care be needed? You may need to arrange for school personnel to assist you.
- Can the parent travel to school? You may need to arrange for transportation, find an alternate site for the meeting in the parents' community, or conduct a home visit.
- How familiar is the parent with the school campus? You may need to arrange for an escort to guide parents to your classroom or meet at the front office.

Generally, at the initial meeting, you will want to ask questions that elicit information about parents' ideas, expectations, values, aspirations, and attitudes associated with their children's schooling. Other questions can help you explore their child's learning styles, general preferences and dislikes, and aspects of their physical, mental, emotional, and social development. (The questions outlined in Figure 4.3 help solicit information about the four modes of communication, interests, and educational aspirations.) This background information will contribute greatly to the effectiveness of your teaching. You can ask different questions in subsequent meetings, knowing that each meeting will enhance your existing background knowledge about the child. And don't forget to allow time for parents to also ask their own questions or to voice their concerns. The objective is to determine the student's strengths and areas needing academic support.

Always begin your meeting with a friendly greeting. Many Latino parents will appreciate a friendly tone of voice, direct eye contact, a firm handshake, and any attempt to use Spanish. Learn familiar phrases like these:

- *Mucho gusto.* (Nice to meet you.)
- *Buenos días.* (Good day.)
- *¿Cómo está?* (How are you?)
- *Bienvenidos.* (Welcome.)

- *Pásenle.* (Come on in.)
- *Yo soy* ______. (I am ______.)
- *Este es nuestro salon.* (This is our classroom.)

In subsequent parent–teacher meetings, take opportunities to discover parents' perspective about their role in their children's schooling. Figure 4.4 includes open-ended questions about child-rearing practices in the home. Asking these kinds of questions is important because parental responses can clarify or support practices with positive outcomes for children. For instance, when a Latina mother mentions that she

FIGURE 4.4
Questions About Child-Rearing Practices

What behavior would you like to see in your child?	*¿Qué tipo de comportamiento le gustaría ver en su hijo(a)?*
How do you discipline your child?	*¿De qué forma disciplina a su niño(a)?*
How do you correct your child's behavior?	*¿Cómo corrige el comportamiento de su hijo(a)?*
How do you let your child know his or her behavior is acceptable?	*¿Cómo le informa a su hijo(a) si él/ella tienen buen comportamiento?*
What are your expectations for your child?	*¿Cuáles son las expectativas que usted tiene para su niño(a)?*
What chores does your child have?	*¿Qué deberes, tareas, o quehaceres tiene su hijo(a)?*
What does your child do when you shop, cook, or maintain the household?	*¿Qué hace su niño(a) cuando van de compras, cocinan, o cuidan la casa?*
Describe any group family activities.	*Describa cualquier actividad que hacen en familia.*
How much TV does your child watch?	*¿Cuánta television ve su hijo(a)?*
What are your child's favorite meals?	*¿Cuáles son las comidas favoritas de su niño(a)?*
What are your child's favorite snacks?	*¿Cuáles son los bocadillos favoritos de su hijo(a)?*
What kinds of meals and snacks do you prepare for your child?	*¿Qué tipos de comida y bocadillos prepara usted para su niño(a)?*
Who cares for your child when you are not available?	*¿Quién cuida a su hijo(a) cuando usted no está disponible?*
What are some of the responsibilities assigned to your child?	*¿Cuáles son algunas de las responsabilidades que le asigna a su hijo(a)?*
What are some of the values that you teach your child?	*¿Cuáles son algunos de los valores que le enseña su niño(a)?*

never takes her children to the library because they prefer watching television, you can comment on how visiting the library to check out books supports reading skills that are highly valued at school. And when a Latino father does not see the point of taking his youngsters to play in the park, you can comment on how play reinforces cognition and how exercise benefits motor development.

As you end each meeting, emphasize that (1) parents are the most important teachers their children will have, (2) their involvement at school is valued, and (3) there are many advantages to participating in the educational process. At some point, mention that parent involvement ultimately supports teachers in meeting the needs of their children. Provide concrete examples of how parents can become involved at your school.

Latino Parents' Views of Teachers

Generally speaking, teachers hold highly respected roles within Latino communities. Some Latino cultures value education so much that they inherently believe that the teacher has the sole privilege of and responsibility for making academic-based decisions for their children. After all, teachers speak and write perfectly in English, they have earned a university education, and they make a fine living educating others. Many parents consider that their own contribution entails providing a home for their child, securing their child's well-being, getting the child ready for school, and ensuring homework is completed.

In this situation, Latino parents wholeheartedly trust the decisions that teachers make and defer to them on all matters associated with their children's education. Many Latino parents may accept teacher-driven decisions based on a lack of knowledge about the U.S. school system and on their own limited schooling and their belief that educators possess the expertise needed to make educational decisions. Parents may also believe that they are underprepared to question individuals with authority, or they may feel vulnerable when having to interact with school personnel who create language barriers and express negative attitudes.

In sum, the degree of respect that Latino parents hold for educators may be so profound that they will rarely judge or contradict a teacher's intentions and actions. Therefore, it is important that the school campus exude a spirit of respect and inclusivity in order to establish opportunities to interact with English language learners and their families. A school should court parents and convince them of their vital role in a partnership anchored in their child's academic success. This means valuing all parents, regardless of language background, occupation, economic status, or immigration status.

TAKE **ACTION**

- Familiarize yourself with your district protocols for identifying and evaluating the language abilities of English language learners in your classroom.
- Find out who the members of the school committee are and how decisions are made about student placements.
- Look for evidence of affirming signage and icons around your school and classroom that welcome parents.
- Talk with parents as frequently as possible, such as when they drop off or pick up their children; call parents to say hello, take advantage of casual encounters in the hallway, and keep in touch by sending notes.
- Find out what other teachers do to organize and conduct meetings with parents.
- Find out what the school policies are for conducting parent meetings.

5

Using Cultural Knowledge for Asset-Based Instruction

In earlier chapters we have referred to an "asset-based model" of instruction, and in this chapter we elaborate on that idea and provide guidance in creating instructional opportunities that value Latino culture by using it as a resource. An asset-based model enables teachers to acknowledge, respect, and integrate the knowledge that Latino parents possess and have shared with their children since birth—including their native language. Working with the spectrum of different backgrounds and experiences represented by the students in their classrooms, teachers are encouraged to incorporate these assets in everyday instruction, making it more authentic, relevant, and engaging to the child. This approach sets the stage for increasing the child's academic potential.

Understanding Language Learning

As we noted in Chapter 3, one of the primary assets that students bring to the classroom is language. Language learning is a complex, slow, and laborious cognitive process. Young children cannot describe the challenges and complexities they encountered in learning their first language (Bialystok, 2007). Language experts agree with Pinker (1995) that typically developing English-speaking children who are monolingual take 5 years to learn the basic structure of the language (birth to kindergarten), 5 years to master complex grammar and subtleties (grades 1 through 5), and 10 years to establish a rich vocabulary (grades 6 through university sophomore level). This means that U.S. schools are systematically designed to enable students to master English within 20 years.

Research has established the vital role of the native language when learning English as a second language (Cummins, 2000; Genesee, Lindblom-Leary, Saunders, & Christian, 2006). For this reason, it is critical to provide English language learners with qualified teachers who can provide adequate language support and resources so that students can achieve academically. According to Cummins (2000), to attain proficiency in the native language, the bilingual person must be able to manipulate deep knowledge of vocabulary, grammar, syntax, and the social use of language (pragmatics). Young English language learners, however, typically do not have the opportunity to learn Spanish at high levels of proficiency if their schooling experience starts in the United States (Thomas & Collier, 2002). In other words, because U.S. schools offer limited opportunities to develop multilingualism, English language learners do not have the privilege of studying their native language for 20 years, as is common for mastering English. Attaining high proficiency in Spanish is also challenged by policies that require children to learn English as soon as possible, even at the risk of losing the native language (what is known as subtractive bilingualism). This is a typical outcome across the United States. The critical shortage of certified bilingual education and ESL teachers also contributes to the loss of the native language. Students who speak two languages quickly realize that schools do not support bilingual development.

Today, some English language learners do have the opportunity to develop high levels of proficiency in both Spanish and English through bilingual education programs by way of "maintenance" models and "two-way, dual-language immersion" models. But these programs are not widespread.

Given this situation, parents have an important role to play. They can support their child's learning English by sustaining the development of the native language at home. Duke and Purcell-Gates (2003) found that Latino children engaged in rich literacy experiences at home, with parents engaging their children in multiple literacy-related activities on a daily basis. The modeling of literacy practices in the home underscored parents' commitment to a partnership between the home and the teacher. Duke and Purcell-Gates found that home and school settings used common texts such as labels, signs, informal texts, messages, maps, lists, magazines, songs, calendars, and schedules, among others.

Linking Home Learning to School Learning

The fact that parents are children's first teachers implies that they influence their children in important ways throughout their lives. As mentioned in Chapter 1, parents teach children lifelong values, beliefs, customs, and everything else that helps the child make sense of the world. Children bring to school what they have learned from home. From the teachers' perspective, recognizing parents' ability to teach their children is a crucial step in valuing parents as partners. Often, however, parents are unaware of how to stimulate their child's academic learning. A lack of understanding of curriculum standards, instructional objectives, and the effect of assessments on their child's achievement limits the potential for creating a bridge between school learning and home activities. Thus it is the teacher's responsibility to share ideas with parents that will enable them to support academic learning at home. For example, parents can—

- Watch educational programs with their children in either Spanish or English. Parents can ask their child to explain what he or she learned or to elaborate on the ideas presented in the program. The child can also summarize, make predictions, and discuss character roles and traits.
- Select age-appropriate music that their children can listen to. They can then ask their children to interpret the lyrics, which expands current understanding. The parent can also ask children to add to the lyrics or to write their own song.
- Take their children to the local public library and explore the many learning opportunities available there. For example, not only can they have their children check out books, they can read together, conduct research using the computer, participate in story time, and read newspapers and magazines. If necessary because the environment is unfamiliar, teachers can meet parents and their children at the library to guide them.
- Turn routine shopping trips into a learning opportunity. At the grocery store, for example, parents can have their children help them select fruits and vegetables, drawing their attention to features like shapes, color, quality, pricing, nutritional value, and so forth. They can also ask the child to estimate the cost of what was purchased at the store. Children can also participate in comparison shopping of similar brands of foods or products, or estimate the savings by shopping at a discount store.
- Ask their children what they learned at school, probing each day about specific skills and concepts learned in class and then discussing why these skills and concepts matter. In this way, parents model their own interest in learning when they

read, calculate household expenses, do their own "homework" (such as paying bills, writing letters, checking their children's homework), watch documentaries or educational programs, and so forth.

- Use the information teachers provide about free community events. Parents can take their children on a nature walk (near a creek or a local park), visit a museum on free-admission day, attend a citywide festival, or take advantage of free tutoring at a church or local hall.

Here are some ideas for teachers. As a teacher, you can—

- Create interest surveys to administer to students that yield information about their homes, neighborhoods, and community and the learning opportunities that each offers.
- Identify public libraries, parks, and recreational centers within the school community and inform parents about the activities they can pursue at those locations.
- Identify businesses that offer learning opportunities. For example, Home Depot and Lowes often sponsor free workshops that teach children how to make toy boats and cars, birdhouses, spice racks, and other items; and Borders and Barnes & Noble frequently host children's authors and storytellers.
- Use resources that list community events (such as Spanish-language newspapers, Spanish-language radio stations, and church bulletins).

Connecting the school curriculum to children's cultures and experiences in an asset-based approach requires that you get to know your students and learn about their home cultures (McIntyre, Rosebery, & Gonzalez, 2001)—a point that we have emphasized in earlier chapters but that bears repeating. Acquiring knowledge about the different cultures represented in your classroom and learning about individual students' experiences help you develop meaningful activities for your students.

Tapping Students' Interests

Knowing what interests and motivates your students and using this information to design and deliver instruction is another example of an asset-based approach. One way to gain this knowledge, as noted in the previous list, is by conducting an interest survey. Obviously, you will have to accommodate any language needs, which may include using a translator, having a bilingual education aide gather the information, or having a Spanish-speaking parent volunteer administer the survey. (Use Figures 5.1 and 5.2 as your guide.) The survey can be extended through various projects, such as having the children illustrate a book about themselves, create a posterboard presentation with magazine cutouts about themselves, make a picture cube, or fill a box with things (or pictures of things) that are important to them.

FIGURE 5.1
Survey Questions for Intermediate Students

Which subject is your favorite? Why?	*¿Cuál es tu materia favorita? ¿Por qué?*
Which subject is your most challenging? Why?	*¿Cuál es la materia que se te hace más difícil? ¿Por qué?*
If you could study one specific topic this year, what would that topic be?	*Si pudieras estudiar un tema específico este año, ¿cuál sería?*
What are some activities that you enjoy doing in school?	*¿Cuáles son algunas actividades que te gusta hacer en la escuela?*
What are some activities that you enjoy doing after school?	*¿Cuáles son algunas actividades que te gusta hacer después de la escuela?*
What are the goals you would like to set for yourself this school year?	*¿Qué metas te has puesto a tí mismo este año?*
How can your teacher support you in reaching these goals?	*¿Cómo puede ayudarte tu maestro(a) a alcanzar esas metas?*
What else would you like your teacher to know about you?	*¿Qué más te gustaría que supiera tu maestro(a) de tí?*

One way to connect English language learners' interests to instruction is to assess prior knowledge by asking, "What do you know about...?" "What can you tell me about...?" and "What do you think about...?" Listening carefully to children's responses can provide you with deeper insight about a child's cognition, knowledge, perspectives, and cultural notions. It is then your responsibility to craft a meaningful connection between the student's contribution and the academic topic or concept you will be teaching.

Students' responses are also beneficial because they can remind teachers that despite commonalities among cultural groups, it is important to remain aware of and develop sensitivity toward individual differences and to find ways to connect teaching to students as individuals. Doing so involves thinking about the role of culture in the classroom. When planning instruction, ask yourself the following questions:

FIGURE 5.2
Survey for Younger Students and Non-English Speakers

All About Me	***Todo Acerca de Mí***
My nickname:	*Mi apodo:*
My best friend:	*Mi mejor amigo(a):*
My best subject:	*Mi mejor materia en la escuela:*
My worst subject:	*Mi peor materia en la escuela:*
My favorite movie:	*Mi película favorita:*
My favorite store:	*Mi tienda favorita:*
My favorite park:	*Mi parque favorito:*
My favorite snack:	*Mi comida/bocadillo favorito:*
My favorite song:	*Mi canción favorita:*
My favorite TV or movie star:	*Mi estrella (actor/actriz) favorito/favorita:*
My favorite toy:	*Mi juguete favorito:*
My favorite place:	*Mi lugar favorito:*
My favorite book:	*Mi libro favorito:*
My favorite story:	*Mi historia favorita:*
My hero:	*Mi héroe:*
Whenever I have play time I like to:	*Cuando tengo tiempo de jugar, me gusta:*
________________ makes me happy.	________________ *me hace feliz.*
If I had a birthday party, I would have it ________________. I would invite:	*Si tuviera una fiesta de cumpleaños, la tendría en ________________. Invitaría a:*
If I could go anywhere in the world, I would go to:	*Si pudiera ir a cualquier lugar en el mundo, iría a:*
When I grow up I'm going to be a(n):	*Cuando crezca, quiero ser:*
I need help with:	*Necesito ayuda con:*

- How have parents socialized their children? Is the student an active participant or a passive recipient of information?
- What communication styles do parents use (verbal and nonverbal)? Do students make eye contact with their teachers, or do they look down as a sign of respect toward adults?

- How have parents taught children to show understanding or agreement? Do students nod their head only to be polite or only when they understand?
- How have parents modeled accomplishing tasks? Do students prefer to work individually, in cooperation with others, or in competition?
- How have parents provided instructions or commands at home? Do students prefer direct, explicit instructions or commands or to be given choices to problem-solve on their own?
- How have parents' aspirations for their children varied based on gender? Does one gender tend to dominate classroom discussions and activities?
- How comfortable are parents in expressing differences of opinion with school professionals? Are students' demeanors relaxed, timid, submissive, or always wanting to please the teacher?

The answers to these questions—many of which you will have learned through your meetings and informal conversations with parents, as described in Chapter 4—can help you make appropriate adaptations and modifications to make lessons meaningful. For additional insight, you can use the questions in Figure 5.3 to foster ongoing conversations with students by addressing familiar topics and asking them to talk about themselves.

Other opportunities to spark conversations and to get to know your students as individuals may emerge simply by reminding yourself that students do not enter the classroom feeling the same way every day and that circumstances in their lives may positively or negatively affect their learning. It is important to be aware of and sensitive to students' frequently shifting needs, and one way to do this is to create the time and space for children to share what may be going on in their lives. You can create your own procedural rules and boundaries for these types of activities while still enabling children to express their thoughts and feelings. For example, Mrs. Martinez, a 2nd grade teacher, established a classroom routine that she called "News and Blues." After morning announcements, she allotted 5 to 10 minutes for students to share good or sad experiences. This activity not only promoted classroom community but also enabled the teacher to adjust her instructional delivery, as appropriate. Mrs. Martinez also found herself applying her behavior management program in more sensitive ways in consideration of what the children had reported. She extended this activity by asking students to write a journal entry when given the following prompt: "Today I am feeling... because... /*Hoy me siento... porque....*"

FIGURE 5.3
Questions to Spark Student Discussion

What do you do when you get home?	*¿Qué haces cuando llegas a casa?*
What do you like to do on the weekend?	*¿Qué te gusta hacer durante el fin de semana?*
What did you do this weekend?	*¿Qué hiciste este fin de semana?*
Who do you play with the most?	*¿Con quién te gusta jugar?*
What do you play?	*¿A qué te gusta jugar?*
If you could have any pet, what would it be?	*Si pudieras tener cualquier mascota, ¿qué escogerías?*
If you could change one rule at school, what would it be?	*Si pudieras cambiar una regla de la escuela, ¿qué sería?*
If you were in charge of the world, what would be your first rule?	*Si tú estuvieras a cargo de todo el mundo, ¿cuál sería tu primera regla?*
How does your mom (or caretaker) make your favorite meal?	*¿Cómo prepara tu mamá (o la persona que te cuida) tu comida favorita?*
What's your favorite candy and why?	*¿Cuál es tu dulce favorito y por qué?*
What's your favorite toy and why?	*¿Cuál es tu juguete favorito y por qué?*
What are your favorite shows and why?	*¿Cuáles son tus programas favoritos y por qué?*
What's your favorite sport?	*¿Cuál es tu deporte favorito?*
What's the happiest day of your life?	*¿Cuál ha sido el día más feliz de tu vida?*
Tell me the many reasons why you love your mom, dad, sister, grandmother, etc.	*Dime las muchas razones por las que quieres a tu mamá, papá, hermana, abuela, etc.*
What do you do in the summer?	*¿Qué haces en el verano?*

Creating a Language-Rich Environment

As we mentioned earlier, Latino students' ability to speak one or two languages is a linguistic asset and a component of their human capital. Caregivers, family, and community members have nurtured students' linguistic repertoire since birth. At home, young children have also observed and have learned about the connection between language and literacy across languages. For example, a young Latino child who speaks only Spanish uses environmental print when selecting a favorite box of cereal or identifying McDonald's, Pizza Hut, or KFC well before learning to read in either language.

Oral language can be nurtured at home in many ways, such as responding to children's questions about what they see, hear, or think. Characters or subject matters they have heard or read about can be topics for conversation. An example of the latter situation occurred one day when Andrea and her aunt were sitting at the kitchen table discussing peaches. The aunt offered Andrea a peach, but the girl declined, saying that she did not like peaches because of their fuzz. Her aunt cut a slice and asked her to taste it; Andrea did and liked it. The child then shared a story that she had read in class. She remembered that the character, a mouse, did not want to taste certain fruits because of their appearance, and she retold the story as she continued to eat the peach. She had made a connection between her immediate experience and an earlier literacy event.

Classroom instruction can support the development of children's language when the learning environment is rich in print and other forms of language. In these classrooms, Latino students have access to good language models as well as meaningful and comprehensible instruction (Kirkland & Patterson, 2005). To create such learning environments for Latino English language learners, consider the following ideas (and note that each suggestion includes a counterpart for parents to engage in with their children):

Create a print-rich environment. In addition to providing a variety of print materials, you can label classroom objects in English and Spanish. For example, signage could clearly designate the Writing Center/El Centro de Escritura, Reading Area/El Area de Lectura, and Teacher's Corner/El Rincón de la Maestra. Engaging students in the labeling is a worthwhile activity in itself.

Encourage parents to label objects around the house for their children who are at the early stages of literacy development. Parents can also contribute literacy materials that can be added to the classroom library. Inform parents that reading letters aloud to children, reading during religious services, clipping coupons, using newspaper circulars to shop for items, and using merchandise catalogs support language and literacy development.

Develop children's vocabulary continuously. Try the "preview, use, and review" approach. Expose children to a variety of words by previewing vocabulary they will be using. Students can use the words to write stories and to complete literacy assignments. Review these orally and post them on a theme-based bulletin board. Providing vocabulary and context for use enables students to learn definitions in meaningful ways. Reproducibles A.6a and A.6b in Appendix A can help with this strategy.

Parents can engage students in word play by rhyming words. Riddles and tongue twisters target vocabulary development and can be culture and Spanish language specific. Other culture- and language-specific activities that parents can do with children include reading poetry, teaching nursery rhymes, engaging children in role-playing, and playing charades. Parents can also use illustrations in picture books to enhance vocabulary development.

Conference with students. As mentioned earlier, teachers can learn from listening to students. Make time for individual student conferences in which you have conversations about stories they have written. For example, imagine that you assigned an essay about an invention for the future. You could ask, "Are there any similar inventions today?" "Who will benefit the most from your invention?" "How will you sell your invention?" You could also ask questions that clarify students' understanding of the English language. For instance, "Why did you put a punctuation mark in front of the sentence?" Or, "Where would you put the stress mark on this English word?" Conferencing is also beneficial because it provides English language learners with the opportunity to practice their new language in a nonthreatening environment with someone they trust.

Having parents listen to children's thoughts and ideas can motivate the children's language development. Parents can conference with their children in various ways. They can (1) ask their children to describe their drawings, sparking conversations about their art; (2) ask about stories the children have written and books they have read; and (3) read and reread familiar texts with their children.

Assign children to tell stories. Storytelling requires that children remember a story that is meaningful to them and orally relate it to others (sometimes adding a physical dimension through hand gestures, dramatic or dance performances, or puppetry). In both instances, students get to practice their receptive and expressive language skills. You can assign students to ask their elders to share a story from their home country. To extend this assignment, students can illustrate their story in a book or storyboard. These could easily be tailored so that the students continue the story or revise it with a modern-day twist.

Parents can recount daily events to their children as a way to engage them in developing listening skills, attending to details, and responding to story events. This engagement with stories parallels school-related literacy tasks. Additionally, parents can invite their children to invent their own stories or to create new endings to familiar stories. Parents can also guide children to incorporate details, descriptive language, and imagery through modeling and by asking questions.

Build a multicultural and diverse classroom library. Expand your library collection by adding books that are award-winning literature as well as those that reflect the authentic experiences of Latinos. Include books that represent different ethnic groups and that address issues of socioeconomic status, class, gender, and social inequities. It will also be important to include books that target the experiences of immigrant children and learning English as a second language. Refer to Appendix D for a list of children's books that can help get you started.

Parents can contribute ideas for books, magazines, and other materials written in Spanish to include in the classroom library. They can also share these reading materials through read-aloud activities in the classroom (the books listed in Appendix D are in both Spanish and English). Additionally, parents can create a book that reflects their own diverse experiences, which can be written or illustrated as a storyboard.

Using Parents to Augment Instruction

As the previous section suggests, Latino parents of English language learners have many skills and talents that school personnel can tap. In fact, they likely have knowledge and understandings of many of the topics covered in the curriculum. Consider these examples of how some teachers have used Latino parents in their classroom to augment lessons:

- One 3rd grade teacher asked members of students' families to share their knowledge of the flora and fauna found in their home countries when the students were learning about regional habitats.
- A 4th grade teacher asked a father to share some of the folktales of his country when the students were learning about folktales from around the world.
- A 5th grade teacher asked a mother to show the class how to make flan and sopapillas when the students were learning about standard units of measurement.
- A kindergarten teacher asked a parent to contribute artifacts from her home country when the students were learning the alphabet. They later assembled an alphabet book of the artifacts.

Gay (2000) and Ladson-Billings (1992) have discussed the importance of using culturally relevant curriculum materials; and Banks (1993) has shown how the use of such materials can strengthen students' self-esteem as they see, read, write, and learn about contributions made by their own ethnic group to the history and culture of the United States. A specific example underscores this point. At one Core Knowledge School (Core Knowledge Foundation, 1999), a 2nd grade bilingual teacher, Mrs. Rios, incorporates her students' experiences into the topics they are studying. Although most of the students in her class are children of Mexican immigrants, some have parents who emigrated from Guatemala. When it was time to study immigration, Mrs. Rios knew that her students were highly familiar with the topic. She decided to incorporate narratives and biographies to expand her students' understanding of reasons why many people migrate to the United States. She engaged students in a "family tree" project, which required them to interview their family members and to trace their roots to the lands from which they came. She also encouraged parents to record their stories to document actual immigration experiences. Students collected the oral histories and published the collection in a class book entitled *Nuestras Historias* (Our Stories). This project afforded the students opportunities to draw interdisciplinary connections as they read and wrote about diverse peoples' immigration experiences.

You can use Reproducible A.7 as a planning guide for how to use Latino parents to augment your lessons.

Involving Parents in Classroom Activities

You can create opportunities for Latino parents to volunteer in the classroom. The vested interest that parents develop as they observe and participate in classroom activities will support their child's academic achievement. However, it is important to recognize that not all families can participate equally. Different families' circumstances, such as work schedules or child care concerns, may prevent some Latino parents from visiting their children's classroom as frequently as others. For this reason, it is advisable to think of other creative ways for children to extend their learning beyond school. If parents cannot help children with their homework because of time constraints or because the child's caretaker does not understand school assignments, you can use some of the following ideas to encourage participation:

Audio recordings for homework. Provide weekly homework assignments in reading in a family-friendly format. The stories that children read in class can be recorded for students to take home and practice. The campus leadership team may be able to fund devices for parents to check out and use at home (using a grant). The recordings can include a story the child read, relevant information the parents must know, and instructions for how to help the child complete the homework. Having a recorded story gives students the opportunity to listen to it many times. For parents who may be nonreaders, this approach also provides a format in which they can access the same information their children are being exposed to at school.

Literacy backpack. Provide activities for parents to work on at home with their children through a literacy backpack—a backpack filled with books in the parents' language that individual children take home each night. The backpack can contain reading material as well as literacy-related activities to be completed after reading or discussing the book. These kinds of activities encourage parents and children to engage in conversations that help develop children's vocabulary, which is one of the best predictors of reading achievement (Catts & Kamhi, 1999). Refer to Appendix D for suggested titles to include in literacy backpacks.

Family involvement through reading. Create a system in which parents have the opportunity to sign up every Friday to visit their child's classroom. Parent volunteers can read a picture book to children in the younger grades and participate in reading aloud with older students. Those who do not speak English can be encouraged to read in their native language so that all students are exposed to languages other than English as an enrichment experience. For parents with limited reading skills who may be hesitant to participate in this activity, you can suggest other language-related alternatives such as singing or storytelling. While your students are studying literature genres, for example, you can invite a parent to talk to them about "El Cucuy" (The Boogeyman) and "La Llorona" (The Weeping Woman), which are popular legends in the Latino community. After parents work with the class, students can ask questions or offer comments. This simple routine can help parents feel they are part of the students' learning community. You may also expand this activity or a similar one to involve parents of Latino English language learners throughout the school campus. In the case of the parent who shared legends with her child's class, for instance, she could be encouraged to work with other parents to identify storytellers in the community who could share stories with the whole school. The campus leadership team could also provide supports for a storytelling festival where students from all grade levels could select their favorite story, memorize it, and orally share it with others in the school community.

Another way for schools to involve families is to develop programs in which parents and teachers work together on strategies they can use to help children. The following example illustrates a collaborative action research project in which a group of 1st grade teachers participated. They first identified a need for greater involvement of parents in reading to their children and then developed a program to fulfill that need. In the program, which they called *Families Involved in Reading Succeed Together* (FIRST), they taught reading strategies to parents. First, the teachers modeled how to read aloud to a child, and then they taught the parents how to generate questions they should ask while reading. Parents were then paired up with their child and given time to practice. With help from funds received through the Center for Teaching Excellence at Eastern

New Mexico University (http://education.enmu.edu/cte/index.shtml), families who participated weekly received incentives in the form of books for children to take home. Throughout the six weeks that this program was in effect, the teachers shared information with parents about what and how to read to their children. At the end of the project, teacher-researchers reported positive changes in the reading behaviors of the participating families and children. Likewise, families reported that they had learned how to read more and better to their children. One mother stated:

> *Yo sé lo importante que es que mi hijo sepa leer. Lo que no sabía es que yo también debo leer con él para ayudarlo. Deberían tener más programas como éste donde uno aprende de cómo los maestros esperan que uno trabaje con el niño.* (I know how important it is for my child to know how to read. What I did not know is that I too should help him read. They should have more programs like this one, where one learns how teachers want us to work with our child.) (Foster, Aguero, Harrison, & Delgado, 1999, p. 9)

A teacher stated:

> I've noticed parents who participated in our workshops are now coming to us more to ask about books they can read with their child. One of the parents even asked me where she could get cheap books for her kid to read and mentioned they had started a library at home! (Foster et al., p. 9)

Academic and behavioral folders. Maintain a folder to help you track each student's behavior during the school year. These behavior logs are an excellent way to communicate with families on a daily basis. Notes written in the folder may include smiley faces to indicate that students made good choices throughout the day; this kind of code is easy to understand. At other times it may be necessary to provide more in-depth information for parents. For example, it is important to communicate when students break rules and how you handle specific situations in class. If you have sent a series of negative notes over the course of a few days, an explanation may help parents understand your observations in the classroom. Notes can also encourage parents to conference with you, and they can prompt parents to speak directly to their child about the issues described in the note. The parent's action exemplifies teamwork within the home-to-school partnership. Through this partnership, you and the parent can develop a plan of action. Reproducible A.8a is a note that you can send to parents when a conference is warranted (with a Spanish version provided in Reproducible A.8b).

Behavioral folders can also become student based and interactive. That is, instead of you explaining incidents that happen at school, students have the opportunity to narrate specific accounts to their parents. More important, this kind of activity is conducive to reflective writing, which promotes children's understanding of being accountable for their own actions and choices. When parents need to transmit a message to you, they can write in the log as well. Notes may range from "Please send homework" to "I'd like to discuss my child's grades with you."

Three-way conferences. Teachers simply do not have the time to conference with parents every day, and so it is advisable to document situations judged as important to share with parents when the opportunity for a face-to-face conference becomes available. Parent–teacher–student conferences help students understand that their actions can have positive and negative consequences. Commonly, parents receive phone calls inviting them to attend a conference to discuss their child's misbehavior or poor academic performance. (Use Reproducibles A.8a and A.8b to invite parents for a conference.) To help develop self-advocacy in young people, you can encourage students to first give their perspective on whatever the issue might be. You and the parents can express yourselves afterward. If it is necessary to intervene either socially or academically, you, the student, and the parents can collectively come up with the best solution for whatever the situation might be. Parents may also request conferences to seek your advice on how to work with their children. One teacher recalled the following situation:

> A mother came to the conference, practically in tears, asking me what I thought she should do with her daughter who was disrespectful and disobedient at home. I was shocked at the parent's description of the student's home behavior and explained that she acts just fine at school. Later, I shared some of her daughter's worries or frustrations that she had expressed to me. Together we discussed possible causes and solutions to her daughter's tumultuous behavior at home.

Conferences are not only about giving parents graded progress reports on their child; they are also opportunities for teachers and parents alike to seek each other out for advice and support, which ensures that the child continues to grow socially and emotionally. And, of course, you can also hold conferences to recognize a student's achievements, which are something to celebrate.

Remembering the Multiple Intelligences

The underpinning of Howard Gardner's (1993) theory on multiple intelligences is that all children manifest intelligence in a variety of ways. This theory frames an asset-based and effective approach to teaching English language learners because it recognizes that every child has a unique way of processing information, problem solving, and understanding the world through individual abilities, strengths, and competencies. Moreover, English language learners have the capacity to solve problems or to create products that are valued in one or more cultural settings (Smith, 2008).

It may be advisable to inform parents about how multiple intelligences are manifested (see Figure 5.4), because many Latino parents may not know about their significance. Explain that multiple intelligences are critical components of your instruction because they are a way to foster critical thinking and they allow opportunities for students to demonstrate their learning in different ways. By sharing with parents what you know about the multiple intelligences, they can structure how their child spends time outside of school. Parents are more likely to seek ways to nurture their child's intelligences when they know how to do so. And they are more likely to challenge their children when they know the kinds of questions to ask. Reproducibles A.9a and A.9b are letters to parents explaining the multiple intelligences, with suggestions for how to coach their children within the respective frameworks.

FIGURE 5.4
Gardner's Multiple Intelligences

Intelligence	Displayed by Students Who Learn Best . . .
Verbal/Linguistic	Through language and who prefer to communicate with others through listening, speaking, reading, and writing.
Logical/Mathematical	By solving problems and reasoning things out.
Visual/Spatial	When information is represented visually.
Bodily/Kinesthetic	Through action and hands-on activities.
Musical	When their sense of rhythm and music is linked through learning.
Interpersonal	When working with others.
Intrapersonal	Through reflection, sharing, and working alone.
Naturalistic	When given the opportunity to figure out how things work.

As described in this chapter, an asset-based approach to instruction relies on collaboration, and collaboration, in turn, requires intentional acts. School practitioners already know the importance of parental involvement, and this makes them responsible for inviting and engaging parents in their child's education. Collaboration assigns parents the responsibility to respond and to reciprocate through their engagement. A collaborative partnership begins with a relationship built on trust, and it requires establishing common goals between the partners that center on the academic achievement of the English learner student.

TAKE **ACTION**

- Inform parents about how home activities can engage their children in learning.
- Get to know students as individuals.
- Administer surveys to solicit English language learners' interests.
- Use survey information to make instruction relevant.
- Inform parents about the value of Gardner's theory of multiple intelligences.

6

Involving Latino Families in Homework

Homework is a contentious topic. Some education experts argue against homework (Bennett & Kalish, 2006; Kohn, 2006; Kralovec & Buell, 2000), noting that research is inconclusive about its benefits and it quite possibly takes away from quality family time. Cooper (1989) reports that homework leads to no significant improvement on test scores at the elementary grades. Others, however, believe that homework produces valuable results (Cooper, Robinson, & Patall, 2006). Ramírez (2003) states that homework is beneficial when it is meaningful, constructive, and authentic and engages the parent and child; when it has been thoughtfully planned; when it can be reasonably completed; and when parents and children believe that it can support academic progress. We encourage parents and school practitioners to pursue the debate to draw their own conclusions. This chapter is based on the premise that school district policies oblige teachers to assign homework, hold them accountable for doing so, and maintain that homework is valuable when it is assigned properly.

Benefits of Homework

Homework can be a constructive tool for getting parents involved in their children's education. Regardless of children's English language proficiency, homework can reinforce or advance their knowledge. When homework's purpose is aligned with a student's ability, the outcome can be advantageous and have affirming long-term effects.

Homework certainly loses its significance and value if children fail to do it, which can happen for various reasons. For English language learners in particular, the reasons can stem from parents' misconceptions about the relevance of completing assignments or not fully understanding how assignments affect their children's education. Consequently, many Latino parents may not enforce homework routines at home. To remedy this situation, teachers and administrators should explain to students and their parents the purpose for assigning homework and outline the anticipated outcomes. Sharing this information with parents can take place during regularly scheduled meetings such as "welcome back to school" orientation sessions, parent–teacher conferences, or PTA (PTO) meetings.

Meeting with Latino parents offers an opportunity to broadly explain the connection between grade-level curriculum standards and homework assignments. Homework assignments also extend activities associated with learning academic content in the classroom to the home. When Latino parents of English language learners understand the rationale and desired outcome, they can motivate their children to complete homework assignments. This understanding enhances the home-to-school connection.

We believe that homework is beneficial for many reasons. When teachers assign homework, it enables another person—whether a parent, an older sibling, or a peer—to reteach a skill or a concept in a different way. In fact, peer teaching is an effective learning strategy. The individual assisting the child can perhaps make the content more comprehensible, for example, by using Spanish, by using different processes to problem-solve, and by using culture-specific ideas to extend critical thinking or make relevant connections. These approaches validate the notion that academic learning can also occur at home when concepts or skills are taught (or retaught) in ways that are meaningful, significant, and culturally relevant. For example, if a teacher assigns a child to write a "how to" essay, parents can teach the child how to make tortillas or a piñata; or if the child has to read 45 minutes a day, parents can help the child select a book on a cultural hero and embellish the story with their own understanding of the character's triumphs.

Homework also helps parents understand the teacher's expectations, motivate their children to apply themselves at school, and reinforce lessons at home to support mastery.

With this kind of home–school connection, teachers can advance through the curriculum assured that children are better prepared to meet grade-level standards. This connection exemplifies the critical contributions that the learning environment of the home can make to school achievement.

When students consistently complete homework, opportunities become available to enrich and extend basic lessons with fun, thought-provoking assignments that deepen knowledge. Teachers can use homework to assess students' mastery of a skill or concept and make adaptations and modifications to their instruction accordingly. Homework is also a great way to communicate to parents about topics or concepts currently being studied, as well as the expectations linked to the curriculum standards used to measure academic performance.

Homework also offers excellent opportunities for parent and child to discuss school-related topics. Parents can talk with their children about the topic linked to the homework assignment, which enables parents to evaluate their child's concept and skill development. Such conversations can be empowering because rather than solely relying on teacher evaluation, parents can make their own assessments. Thus, when a teacher reports that a child has difficulty with phonemic awareness, for instance, the parent can support the child's learning by reciting nursery rhymes in the native language. Parents can also use their own appraisal to ask the teacher about challenges that their child has encountered, request additional homework assignments to support learning gaps, request that the child receive tutoring at school, or secure the services of a private tutor, if warranted. Alternatively, parents can also seek specific enrichment activities to enhance their child's strengths, talents, and aspirations. When parents attend to the learning objectives associated with the homework assignments, they can better understand their child's academic progress and create additional opportunities that enrich the learning.

Well-designed homework is fundamentally structured to benefit the child. Above all, homework helps young children develop study habits, which are critical to their success in later grades. Homework also helps children refine their skills and strengthen their understanding of particular concepts. Children who have not mastered certain grade-level learning objectives can have someone such as an older sibling or a peer use home-based assignments, projects, and reading to enrich their abilities. The time that parents and children spend on completing homework allows them to learn from each other, advancing current knowledge. Additionally, homework assigned in the lower grades prepares young students to expect homework in the upper grades and well into adolescence and beyond the baccalaureate. Once homework routines are established, children learn the importance of time and task management, which are lifelong skills that are useful throughout adulthood. More important, they begin to associate their home with learning.

School districts nationwide have enacted policies that state that homework is an essential component to instruction. See Appendix E to gain perspective about homework policies in school districts across the country. Note that some districts require that students spend specified amounts of time on particular homework assignments, such as reading for 45 minutes daily.

English Language Learners and Homework

When assigning homework, it is important to keep special considerations in mind for English language learners because their language and cultural practices differ from those associated with schooling in the United States. Differences in students' and parents' schooling experiences encompass discipline-related terminology, interpretations and perspectives, and approaches to identifying issues. Consider the following examples:

- In math, problems involving fractions are solved differently in the United States than in Latin American countries. The teacher should be receptive to accepting varying algorithms, which allow for solving math problems in multiple and divergent ways.
- In social studies, Latino students not schooled in the United States may not know about "Honest Abe," the religious and industrious Pilgrims, or the innovative spirit of Ben Franklin. Rather than perceiving this as a serious limitation through a deficit paradigm, teachers should become aware of and accommodate (through an asset-based approach) the knowledge that students may already possess—for example, Benito Juárez, the first indigenous Mexican president, represents honesty and dignity for all; the Mayans invented the concept of zero, and the Aztecs built aqueducts; and Guillermo González Camarena, a Mexican engineer, invented color TV.
- In geography, students may not know about the Grand Canyon, but perhaps they have visited Las Barrancas del Cobre (Copper Canyon, located in the Mexican state of Chihuahua), which is comparable to the Grand Canyon. Moreover, some Latino students may know the Rio Grande as the Río Bravo. Ultimately the teacher is responsible for bridging, communicating, and mediating understanding of different perspectives.

These are powerful examples of respecting diversity and the knowledge that stems from particular cultural backgrounds. The teacher who possesses insight and is able to orchestrate divergent forms of knowledge can create lessons that enrich all students' learning. In other words, all students benefit from learning about values and principles shared by a global society.

The question remains, Why do some Latino English language learners fail to fulfill their homework obligations? Teachers may assume that when children do not complete their homework it is because they chose not to do it rather than considering that the learning objective was not thoroughly taught and needs to be retaught or that the homework assignment was not fully explained. Some children need detailed, repeated explanations on how to best complete their homework, how to neatly arrange their math problems to show their work, how to find a library book from a specific genre, or how to frame their paper's heading. For the many children who are unsuccessful at completing homework assignments (especially the ones with limited parental support, guidance, or motivation), it may be far more appealing to receive a zero grade than to skip TV, video games, and playing outside, all of which offer immediate gratification.

Teachers have many things to think about when assigning homework. For example, many children are not in the habit of doing homework because it is not meaningful to them and they do not understand how it affects their achievement. Teachers have to consider that many Latino children who live in poverty value securing daily sustenance and shelter above completing homework. Moreover, many Latino children from low-income backgrounds may not have a designated place conducive to doing homework, such as a desk or a quiet place to study. Their homes may lack school supplies, books, and encyclopedias or other resources, and their only access to computers may be at the public library. Some children may also be unaccustomed to routines, including a specified time for completing homework, and they may have no one to check on their progress when adult caretakers work two or three jobs to support the family. Under these circumstances, asking children to complete homework assignments is like asking teachers to write a graduate thesis at a rock concert.

Promoting Good Homework Habits

Rather than fault children and their parents for not taking the responsibility to do homework, we advise school practitioners to help them to fully understand the merits of homework. You can use the ideas described in the following sections with any child who consistently fails to complete home assignments. However, the reproducibles for this chapter, available in Spanish as well as English, target Latino English language learners.

Teach Children and Parents the Value of Homework

It is important to formally notify children and parents about the homework policy at your school. Because many Latino parents are not familiar with the U.S. educational system and the nuances associated with classroom instruction, as well as regional influences, they may not fully understand what homework suggests and involves. Latino parents who do not speak, read, or write English face the dilemma of distinguishing varying types of important papers sent by schools (such as applications for reduced-price meals, invitations to PTA meetings, and so forth). This situation is particularly common for families that do not participate in a social network that can offer support in understanding the information sent by schools. Another consideration is that children may not convey information about the homework they have been assigned, remaining tight-lipped because they do not want to burden the family or hamper their own plans for watching TV or playing video games.

Parents who emigrated from countries where the schooling and resources were limited may have never had homework, so they also do not understand its purpose. Some may even believe that the tasks that their children are assigned—for example, to color, draw a picture, make words rhyme, and so on—lack academic merit. Thus it is essential to clearly explain to both children and their parents the purpose that homework fulfills.

As early in the school year as possible—perhaps with the first homework assignment of the year—create a lesson that teaches the children how important homework is for their schooling. In addition to the benefits discussed thus far, stress in a developmentally appropriate fashion that homework does the following:

- Builds students' knowledge of subject matter they have learned at school.
- Helps them master grade-level skills and build upon them.
- Helps their parents assess how they are progressing.
- Helps teachers evaluate the students' needs and adjust their instruction accordingly.
- Allows for children to interact with their parents (for example, they can have their parents review their work, or they can interpret and explain how they completed their work).
- Builds the foundation for lifelong learning because they learn to make time for learning at home.

The overall goal is to help them understand that homework is a significant aspect of their entire education. Once you have discussed the benefits of homework with your students, send a letter home to parents making the same points. Reproducible A.10a (and its Spanish-language counterpart in Reproducible A.10b) is a letter that can be distributed to parents. Also, you can use some of the statements found in Figure 6.1 to make posters and displays for your classroom or the school's parent/community room.

FIGURE 6.1
Phrases to Motivate Students to Complete Homework

Homework is awesome.	*La tarea es fascinante.*
Homework is terrific.	*La tarea es buenísima.*
Homework is great.	*La tarea es excelente.*
Homework builds understanding.	*La tarea ayuda al entendimiento.*
Homework builds your knowledge base.	*La tarea es la base del conocimiento.*
Homework helps you master skills.	*La tarea ayuda a mejorar destrezas.*
Homework helps teachers help you.	*La tarea ayuda a los maestros a ayudarte.*
Homework is time to spend with your parents.	*La tarea es tiempo para pasar con tus padres.*

Inform Children and Parents About Homework Policy

As part of a lesson on homework, inform the students of your policies and procedures. First, indicate how often you expect to assign homework, which may be based on your school district's policy. If appropriate, help your students understand this research-based rule: multiply the grade level by 10 minutes; multiply the grade level by 15 minutes if the assignment requires reading (Cooper, 2007). In other words, a 3rd grade student should have about 30 minutes of homework (or 45 minutes if it includes reading), whereas a 5th grader should have about an hour and 15 minutes of homework if it includes reading. Plan homework around this formula, which should allow for ample time to study for tests or to work on large-scale projects, such as a science fair or an art exhibit.

Next, tell students how you plan to use their homework. Decide when it will be used as part of their grade averages and reflected on their report cards and when it will be used only as your informal diagnostic. Follow with a discussion on when homework is due and point out that studying for tests and quizzes is considered homework too.

Communicate clearly with students, informing them of the consequences linked to incomplete homework assignments. You can work with your students to establish a set of consequences at the beginning of the school year and revisit it periodically thereafter. Some circumstances might justify turning in homework late without penalty; if so, make those clear. Students should also be informed that incomplete assignments may merit a grade of zero or loss of a privilege.

Some innovative teachers use positive reinforcement by offering a "homework pass" or "homework-free evening" to recognize students who consistently complete their homework. One teacher made a "credit card" using her last name, calling it the *Gutierrez Homework Express Card.* Every time the students turned in their homework, she would punch a hole through a mark on their cards. When all of the marks were punched through, the students could trade in the card in place of a homework assignment. Other teachers offer students options. For example, given seven homework assignments at the beginning of the week, students can opt to complete four to fulfill the requirement. The children and their parents are fully informed of this option and decide which assignments to complete based on convenience and interest.

Preparing students to complete their homework assignments can be a natural transition at the end of the school day or class period. It is important to discuss how you will help them get organized before they leave for the day. Explain that you will write the assignments on the board (including subject area, particular resources, page numbers, and special notes), detailing the information you expect from them. Model some examples and answer questions so that students know your expectations. This is also the perfect opportunity for you to let them know that you are looking for neat, complete work and then segue the discussion to explain what it means to be conscientious about homework.

Some schools purchase agendas to help students organize their homework assignments. If students do not have agendas, consider using a homework sheet and folder. Students can use this folder to transport their homework and graded papers for their parents to review. The folder is a valuable tool because the students learn early in the school year that the instructions for completing their homework can be found in one location, and it supports development of the metacognitive skill of self-evaluation as students check their own progress when the graded work is returned. The folder is good for parents because they can establish the habit of asking their children for the homework folder and then help their children complete the assignments as well as ascertain their progress. Additionally, with the efficient use of a homework folder, parents are less likely to be surprised when they receive their children's report cards. Parents can use the homework folder to send their own notes. Reproducible A.11a (and the Spanish version in Reproducible A.11b) is a form you may consider inserting in the folder's pocket; it allows the parent to communicate when the homework is too difficult.

Reproducible A.12a (and A.12b) is another homework sheet that you can use with the homework folder. Distribute a sheet at the beginning of each week and have the students write in the information they need to complete their daily assignments. You can have the students do this at the end of each lesson or at the end of the day. A separate box allows you (or the students) to enter the grade they earned on their homework.

Next, mention how you will collect their homework. Some teachers collect it soon after the students have arrived in the classroom and are settling in; others collect it as they progress through the content areas and review it during or after the respective lessons. Once you have graded the homework, return it promptly so that students (and their parents) can gauge how well they mastered the assignment.

Later in the discussion, be sure to address the responsibilities everyone has, including the following. The students will—

- Clearly write the assignments and directions before they leave for the day.
- Ask questions about the assignments if they are uncertain about something.
- Use the homework sheet (or agenda) as a guide and as a gauge of their own progress.
- Complete homework when it is assigned.
- Articulate to their parents or teachers what they learned.
- Transport messages between the teachers and their parents.
- Take care of their agenda or homework folder and sheet.

The teacher will—

- Create assignments that are challenging, meaningful, and fun.
- Assign homework related to topics introduced thus far.
- Vary the assignments.
- Provide clear directions about the assignments.
- Allow time in the school day for the students to start their homework so there is time for them to ask questions about it.
- Create assignments that require the students to use resources they have at home.

- Grade homework promptly so the students and their parents can measure their progress.

The parents will—

- Arrange for time in the evening for the children to do their homework.
- Insist that their children do homework.
- Guide their children through their homework without providing the answers or doing the work.
- Use the homework sheet as a guide to review their children's work.
- Review graded work with their children.
- Communicate with the teacher when they have some concerns about their children's homework.
- Respond to the teacher's letters.

It is important that both teachers and parents communicate an expectation that students diligently fulfill their homework responsibilities. You can send a letter, such as that in Reproducibles A.13a and A.13b, to parents informing them of the homework policy. The letter, which can be photocopied on the back of the "Homework Is Wonderful" reproducible (A.10a and A.10b) and which has various options, informs parents of your homework policy and your expectations.

Explain Ideal Homework Practices

Explain to students and their parents that there are ideal practices that support the effective completion of homework. At the same time, empathize with individual circumstances that may curb a family's ability to provide any of these ideals. Practices to encourage include the following.

Establish a nightly routine. Tell the students to work with their parents to create homework time that is consistent every school night. The time can be as soon as the children get home from school or sometime after they have rested, relaxed, or played outside. Alternatively, homework time can be later in the evening, before bedtime. The point is to establish a time that is convenient and most efficient for children and their parents alike. The family should institute rules for this time that engender a climate that supports study. Here are some suggestions:

- No TV, video games, or music playing
- No phone calls

- No computer or Internet usage, unless it is for homework
- No friends coming over

Although some of the family members may find these rules unreasonable—especially siblings who have no homework—it is important to stress that the home should be quiet and that family members can pursue quiet activities like drawing or reading during the reserved time.

Find a reasonable place to do homework. Suggest that the family locate an area in the home that is conducive to doing homework—a place that is comfortable, well lit, and free from as many distractions as possible (such as the phone and TV). Kitchen and dining room tables are often ideal because they allow children to spread out their materials. The selected location should be identified as *the* study area where children go to complete their homework.

Supply the homework/study area with resources. Explain to parents that the homework/study area should be stocked with resources like pens, paper, pencils, crayons, scissors, glue, scrap paper, calculators (for checking work), reference materials (like a dictionary and thesaurus), assorted books (including those checked out from the library), and so forth. Children have an easier time completing their homework when the resources they need are in one location. Reproducible A.14a (and A.14b, in Spanish) is a short memo that you can send to parents describing helpful homework resources. For parents who do not have the means to provide these resources, consider sharing any extra supplies you may have. Often, school supplies are on sale at rock-bottom prices at specific times of the year, and you might consider purchasing extras at these times.

Discuss the homework. Students and parents should have a mutual time to discuss homework assignments and review them for accuracy and neatness. This exchange communicates the importance of homework to both students and parents. Parents can even create a homework chart that rewards children for completing their homework successfully. The child can check off doing homework before positive reinforcement activities such as watching TV, playing outside, and so forth, and the parents can use the system to see how well the child is progressing. Reproducible A.15a (and A.15b, in Spanish) is an example of a homework chart that parents can use at home.

(For convenience, the reproducibles mentioned in this chapter are provided as separate documents. Reproducibles A.16a and A.16b combine these elements into one lengthy letter for parents. Distribute these according to your needs.)

As we mentioned previously, some Latino families may not be able to provide any of these ideal practices for completing homework, and it is important to take into consideration the circumstances of individual students to objectively determine why homework assignments may be incomplete. Many factors could be involved, and issues associated with poverty are prime considerations. For example, a child who is homeless may not have access to any private space; a child may be sharing a busy household with extended family members or multiple families, making quiet spaces limited or nonexistent; or families may not have the means to provide the suggested school supplies.

Teach Homework and Study Skills

In addition to learning about the importance and benefits of homework, students need to understand the cognitive elements involved. The act of completing homework helps students to make generalizations about the learning process, which facilitates the transfer of learning from one context to another. In other words, skills that students may learn from completing homework assignments can be applied to learning in the various subject areas as they continue to grow as learners. Teach them specific strategies like previewing the work, carefully reading the instructions, rereading for clarity, and generating reflective questions. Have students identify key words that guide them to follow the instructions correctly. It is critical that students recognize how homework assignments are connected to the lessons presented in class. Suggest that students ask themselves the following questions:

- "How does this assignment relate to what we did in class today?"
- "How does this relate to what we did yesterday or before?"
- "What is the value of doing this assignment?"
- "What is most important in doing this assignment?"
- "How might I use this information in the future?"

Then, teach students to check their work for accuracy and neatness and to give it to parents or older siblings for review.

Consider teaching a separate lesson on study skills for tests and quizzes. The lesson could teach students about effective use of flash cards, highlighting important information, predicting test questions, and so forth.

Carefully Plan for Homework

Rather than assigning homework solely to fulfill district-mandated homework policies, take the time to plan for homework that is relevant to student learning. Steer clear of consistently assigning homework that is—

- Time consuming and offers no authentic value (for example, copying passages from a book or writing spelling words 10 times each).
- Punishment (for example, extra worksheets to complete because the student misbehaved).
- Put together at the spur of the moment.
- Disconnected from curriculum standards or what students are learning (for example, repetitive drills, memorizing facts, and solving redundant problems).

Such homework assignments will likely distress and frustrate both children and their parents.

Moreover, do not expect parents to have expert knowledge of academic content or to be master decoders of instructions that require a certain level of background knowledge. Although teachers may be familiar with topics like whales, Native Americans of the Southwest, Matthew Henson, and other topics commonly taught at a given grade level, parents may be unfamiliar and unprepared to assist their children with any of these topics, among others. Imagine the reaction of parents who are English language learners and lack content and U.S. cultural knowledge.

Instead, create assignments that are relevant to Latino English language learners (see Figure 6.2 for a range of ideas that can be adapted for your class and grade-level assignments). In addition to reading a passage about the lived experiences of African Americans during the civil rights era, students can interview someone in their family who has experienced discrimination or racism. Instead of solving a series of math problems focused on liquid measurement using paper and pencil, ask students to create healthy treats and desserts using cups, ounces, pints, and so forth. To augment a story on produce, ask students to go to the market with their parents and generate a list of as many fruits and vegetables as they see. Active learning consists of meaningful assignments students look forward to completing. And don't forget that tapping different types of intelligences (as discussed in Chapter 5) requires that assignments engage students beyond completing worksheets.

Also, consider assigning homework that is project-based, in which students have to collaborate with one another to fulfill a series of academic tasks (planning, researching, organizing material, presenting findings, evaluating contributions, and so forth). For English language learners, collaborative projects are excellent because they provide opportunities for students to enhance social skills, practice their English as they complete academic tasks, and forge friendships with native English speakers. When assigning projects, keep in mind the following considerations:

FIGURE 6.2
Ideas for Meaningful Assignments

- Create an ad or a commercial.
- Create a TV show or cartoon.
- Design a puppet show.
- Create a children's picture book or comic strip.
- Create and design an award to present to someone.
- Create an idea for a new candy bar.
- Create a photo essay.
- Write a contemporary fairy tale.
- Design a mural.
- Design and implement a survey.
- Record an oral history.
- Create a mobile.
- Design a game.
- Design a learning center.
- Write a letter to a notable figure.
- Design a robot.
- Design a machine that will change the lives of everyone on earth.
- Given a million dollars, how would you improve…?
- Design a family crest after interviewing family members about the history of your family.

• Ensure that the students understand the objectives of the project, which can be easily accomplished by telling them directly or by guiding students to generate meaningful connections.

• Write clearly stated directions that outline the responsibilities that every group member has to complete the project. Rubrics can help students to plan their work toward a specific outcome and to evaluate their progress.

• Ensure that the assignment can be done. If the project is not well planned, students may perceive it to be insurmountable—too difficult or too time consuming. The students may become frustrated and choose not to contribute substantially to the completion of the assignment. The project (and other assignments) should not require the students to use a computer or the Internet if they do not have easy access to them; nor should they be required to post their findings on poster boards that they have to buy if their families cannot afford them. To determine if the students can obtain the resources and supplies needed, the teacher can simply ask, "How would you get… if I wanted you to…?" Or "What are some ways you could… if I wanted you to…?"

- Some students may be able to collaborate with others only during school hours. Consequently, allow time in the school day for students to work together to complete projects. This time also gives you an opportunity to evaluate their progress and guide them accordingly (for example, to nudge them to speak more English or to urge native English speakers to support their peers).
- Ensure that the projects coincide with students' interests. You can use surveys, as discussed in Chapter 5, to identify their concerns, attitudes, aspirations, and beliefs and to determine how to use these in a project. Not surprisingly, English language learners will have their own unique views on current topics and other matters, which you can consider in your planning. If you are short on ideas for a project, have the students initiate their own. Student-generated projects are likely to incorporate their own particular interests.
- Ask the students to solve a real-life problem. For instance, if you want students to learn about civic leaders who were able to enact social change, you could assign students to create a campaign to increase parent involvement at the grade level, to design a "green" program for the school, or to examine community challenges and brainstorm projects for resolving them.
- Vary projects and activities. Although tasks like writing research reports and presenting findings are beneficial, entice the students by integrating a creative component, such as requiring them to create a dance, write a poem, make a game, and so forth. Again, consider the multiple intelligences when developing a range of ideas.

Whether the homework assignment is a simple task or is related to a major project, allow time in the day for the students to begin their homework. Doing so allows them to ask questions about the assignment, and it affords you the opportunity to give them feedback on things like spacing out their math problems and showing their work, or writing within the margins. Also, have an example or a model of the final product available so students can fully understand what the expectations are and what is acceptable.

After the students turn in their homework, grade and return it as soon as possible and use it to guide instruction. Commenting on students' mistakes and commending their accuracy can make for teachable moments. For example, a teacher could say, "I really like the way José showed all his work and solved this math problem. Let's look at what he did. . . ." Or, "Maria wrote something interesting. Would you read your essay, Maria?" Or, "I noticed a lot of common errors in your projects. Let me teach you a way to. . . ." Comments like these also validate that students' work is connected to what they learn, and the recognition that they get is likely to encourage them to complete their homework. In addition, if homework is consistently first-rate, you can tailor your instruction (and future homework assignments) to make it even more challenging.

Last, be sure to praise the students for their efforts or when they are doing homework successfully. Send home positive notes that indicate that you are proud of their work; such messages reinforce the notion that homework is important. (Reproducibles A.17a and A.17b consists of mini certificates that you can send to parents.) Similarly, send notes or progress reports when the need arises, especially when a student turns in substandard work or nothing at all. Because parents often want to know when homework problems arise, it is important to keep them informed of how their children are performing. (Reproducibles A.18a and A.18b are general forms that can be used for such occasions.)

TAKE **ACTION**

- Share your homework policy with your students and their parents.
- Communicate the benefits of homework to students and parents.
- Explain that homework is an important component of lifelong learning.
- Recognize and identify challenges English language learners may encounter when completing homework.
- Recognize your responsibility to facilitate communication and mediate challenges regarding homework.
- Help children and parents understand good homework habits.
- Design relevant homework assignments and projects based on the needs and interests of your students.

7

Identifying Community Assets

Many Latino English language learners come from low-income backgrounds and communities where social services and amenities are lacking. When this is the case, many teachers have difficulty perceiving assets in the form of businesses, churches, and organizations in the school community. Rather than viewing Latino communities as having little to offer schools, teachers need to recognize and seek out the valuable resources that are available and that can contribute to the education of children. This chapter is intended to help teachers build positive relationships within the local school community. Such relationships can influence children's achievement and the welfare of the community as a whole.

Getting to Know the Community

Teachers who work with Latino families of English language learners often do not live in their students' communities. We recommend that school personnel get to know the community where they teach so they can better understand the strengths and needs of the students and families they serve. Once they become familiar with the realities of the world in which their students live, teachers can better understand how social and academic problems are interdependent, so that neither can be attended to in isolation (Shonkoff & Phillips, 2000). Knowledgeable teachers are also better equipped to incorporate authentic experiences into their instruction to make student learning engaging, rather than relying on lessons drawn directly from textbooks or scripted programs that may not interest students. All communities have a particular landscape, geographical setting, and economic profile, and becoming familiar with these elements of the neighborhoods where their students live provides the context for helping teachers to understand the whole child.

Survey the Neighborhoods

One way to get to know a community is to survey the neighborhoods—much as one would do before purchasing a home. Often potential home buyers drive around the neighborhood of interest, research important facts about it, and assess the quality of the schools, choice of grocery stores, and services and amenities such as health care facilities, libraries, and shopping malls. You can use Figure 7.1 as a survey form to record information about the community where your students live. Consider how the information generated by the survey can be useful to parents (location of free health clinics), teachers (location of cultural centers within walking distance of school), children (location of libraries, recreational programs, and other facilities), and school district officials (location of businesses interested in forming school–community partnerships).

As you gather, review, and interpret information about the community, your perspectives may change or broaden. Also, when you invite parents to contribute their own knowledge and interpretations, you'll gain a more comprehensive assessment of the school community. Although we encourage teachers to work with small core groups of parents (to identify their needs and wants, as discussed in Chapter 2), schoolwide committees can address community-based concerns (such as dealing with adults loitering near school, making the school playground available on weekends, landscaping the school grounds). It is important to acknowledge that the contributions parents make emerge from their knowledge as community residents, which may provide new insights.

You can also guide students in generating critical questions based on observations of their own community. Students may identify problems and concerns and even propose solutions to challenges they experience on a regular basis. Other possible academic tasks include composing essays and poetry and creating art related to their community. *Do the Write Thing* (National Campaign to Stop Violence, 2010) is an excellent example of how a community-based violence-prevention program encourages students to discuss, write, and communicate about what they think should be done to reduce youth violence (see www.dtwt.org).

Additionally, administrators can use information gathered about the community to develop campuswide initiatives related to parental involvement and other identified needs. This information can counter the negative perceptions and attitudes of school

FIGURE 7.1
Assessing the School Community

Part 1. Drive within a one-mile radius around the school. Invite a fellow teacher to document the following information.

	What I discovered	How does this affect the families I serve?
Describe the housing within the one-mile radius of the school.		
List the public amenities that you encounter: • Utility companies • Stadiums, museums, theaters • Public pools • Churches • Other schools • Library • Cultural centers • Other		
List the businesses that you encounter: • Gasoline stations • Grocery stores • Hospitals and health facilities • Restaurants • Cinemas • YMCA, gyms, and similar facilities • Repair shops (auto, appliance, etc.) • Other		
Describe your experience driving around the one-mile radius of the school: • Condition of streets, traffic lights, crosswalks (clearly marked?), etc. • Pedestrian flow • Sidewalks • Mass transit, covered bus shelters • Amount of traffic • Any flooding during rainy seasons (or other impediments caused by weather)		

Part 2. Ask school counselors or social workers, or parents at the small-group meetings, to help you identify people, programs, and community connections.

	What I discovered	How does this affect the families I serve?
Identify community leaders: • Leadership roles may be informal or formal, such as representing an institution or a business entity.		
Identify programs within the community: • Identity those that are pertinent to students, their family, or education.		
Identify the community connections that support education.		

practitioners toward Latino parents by broadening views and revealing the complexities that parents encounter in their community. For example, if the school is located in an impoverished community, it may reflect such attributes as—

- Parents who work two or three jobs (part- or full-time) to maintain the household.
- Children who are responsible for waking up and getting to school on their own.
- Children who have responsibilities that sustain the household.
- Insufficient access to hospitals, medical clinics, and physicians.
- Insufficient access to playgrounds and areas where children can play safely.
- Insufficient modes of mass transit.
- Insufficient number of stores.
- Insufficient access to social services.
- Inadequate housing.

You and your colleagues can also get to know the community by participating in a neighborhood walk. At the beginning of the school year at one elementary school, for example, the principal divides faculty into groups and assigns them to walk to a particular block in the surrounding neighborhood. Before studying their block and mapping it, the groups of teachers describe what they think they might see or hear there. As they go on their neighborhood walk, the teachers record what they actually see and report back to the whole school. This exchange allows the faculty to get a big picture of their school neighborhood, to understand the challenges they may face, and to brainstorm ideas for ways to enhance students' physical, academic, social, and emotional development. After participating in a neighborhood walk, one teacher provided the following reflection:

> Sometimes it's just easy to blame parents who do not take their children to the public library or to the park. After this walk, I realized there's no library nearby. The community park is not well kept. This experience got me thinking of ways in which I can contribute more to my students' well-being. Perhaps I can provide more books for them to take home or encourage families to use our school's playground.

A neighborhood walk can also serve as an opportunity for teachers and students to learn together. Studying one's neighborhood is part of any social studies curriculum. Parents can accompany teachers on the walk, and parents new to the community can benefit from the excursion. Reproducible A.19a (and A.19b, in Spanish) is a letter you can send parents informing them of this activity.

Build on Social Networks

In time, young children become aware of wider social networks that exist in the community where they live. They learn about the information resource that exists within their community when they witness the "funds of knowledge" (Moll, Amanti, Neff, & Gonzalez, 1992) that their parents share and exchange with neighbors and others. Many Latino families live near their relatives. A Latino child may live within a short walking distance of grandparents and other extended family members such as aunts and uncles. Also, when Latino families do not have a relative living in the same community or city, they may have a trusting relationship with a neighbor who is considered a surrogate family member (the person may be considered a *compadre* or *comadre,* signifying a status beyond friend). The funds of knowledge shared or exchanged within a family's social network may concern any number of things, such as sewing, baking, car repair, carpentry, plumbing, construction, and translating, among other activities.

Sometimes teachers may be challenged in recognizing funds of knowledge because they are not familiar with the very assets unique to the communities and families they serve (for example, they may not recognize the fund of knowledge that a Latino mother has when she uses the healing properties of herbs to cure her children's aches). You can gain insight about these community assets by asking Latino parents questions such as, "Does your family depend on others for help from time to time?" Or, "Do others depend on your help?" And, "Are there instances of exchanging services with others, such as baby-sitting for car repair?" Answers gathered can help you recognize the strengths that all children, including English language learners, and their families have.

Teachers who function from an asset-based perspective build upon the strengths generated in students' homes and communities and use them in daily instruction (Gay, 2000). For example, Mrs. Shay, a 4th grade teacher who understood the importance of this approach, was aware that in her students' community, several mothers mixed banana peels into the dirt they used to grow rose bushes. When students were learning about different types of soil, Mrs. Shay used this information to start a class discussion on the nutrients that soil needs.

Another way to learn about what happens in students' lives and in their communities is to identify places where families gather and to meet them there informally. Latino families, like most families across the United States, are social and hence gather in the community. Whereas some may picnic in the park, others congregate at church grounds, and still others find the *mercado* ("market square"—a plaza in the vicinity of small stores and restaurants) to be an ideal place to meet relatives and neighbors. One Latino community made their local Wal-Mart the social hot spot on Sunday afternoons; families could shop for their household necessities and then sit and chat with others who were taking advantage of the economical meals the food venders sold.

At one school, a group of Latino mothers would gather near the kindergarten portable unit before picking up their children and converse with each other long after school dismissal. Although their conversations were often about issues central to their lives, they largely talked about their children's schooling. Mrs. Duggins, one of the kindergarten teachers, used this opportunity to ask the mothers to volunteer in the classroom. Some of the mothers in the group started showing up earlier at school and talked while they completed work in Mrs. Duggins's classroom. They shared with Mrs. Duggins some of the experiences that challenged families at their school campus, and she played a critical role in identifying resources to support the families. For example, one of the mothers mentioned that her family was about to become homeless because of financial difficulties. Mrs. Duggins encouraged the mother to visit the school's counselor and social worker, who provided her with information about a program specializing in helping homeless families get permanent housing.

Another way for teachers to increase their visibility in the school's neighborhood is to visit businesses close to where they teach, including restaurants, gas stations, and grocery stores or supermarkets. A teacher at one elementary school reported that she learned the most about her students when talking with their families at places where they just happened to meet each other. The teacher said:

> Collaboration with parents comes easy when they know you are genuinely interested in being a part of their community. As teachers, we have to create the opportunities to participate in our students' lives outside of school. Once in a while, go to a public site such as the same store where your families shop. Show them that you continue to care about them, even after the school bell rings.

Conduct Field Trips and Sponsor Fairs

Identifying local businesses that can support student learning provides opportunities for building school–business partnerships. Teachers, for example, can incorporate a field trip to a bank when learning about the principles of economics or to a garden center when learning about botany. Some teachers have taken children on field trips to local post offices, bakeries, grocery stores, fire stations, and shopping centers to augment their units of study. To capitalize on field experiences, one teacher arranged for her class to go downtown using public transportation. To take the bus, students had to (1) calculate how much money they would need, (2) identify what routes to take, and (3) manage time to get where they were going. In addition to gaining important academic and social skills, the teacher and her students learned about their community as a result of this trip. When field trips are not possible because of costs, time constraints, or risk to children's health and safety (as might be the case when visiting medical clinics, hospitals, or auto repair shops, for example), consider contacting business or professional representatives who might agree to visit the school and answer the children's questions about their respective careers and business operations.

Students in the upper grades (and their parents) may benefit from a business fair held at the school, where business owners could gather to talk to students, families, and teachers about the jobs they do and how to work together to support each other. These kinds of activities are particularly helpful to Latino students who may not have a professional role model at home. At an elementary career fair in one community, the principal invited a Latino engineer to talk to students. When this professional shared his school experiences with the children, they were surprised to find out that he had grown up in a neighborhood similar to theirs. The young engineer talked about challenges he had encountered and explained how he stayed focused to do well in school. In addition to exposing these elementary students to a professional career, this guest speaker encouraged them to explore different kinds of professions and motivated them to pursue higher education.

Having guest speakers from local community businesses at school also presents an opportunity for teachers and administrators to ask the businesses to sponsor activities or to donate goods such as T-shirts for the spelling bee competition, food and supplies for PTA meetings, or funds for a new playground, sports equipment, band instruments, tools for a garden, and other items. One school, for instance, entered a partnership with an insurance company that eventually donated new infant and toddler safety car seats to Latino families. These activities should be carried out with a mutual interest in maintaining a community–school partnership.

Provide After-School Opportunities

Schools can become an integral part of the community when they plan activities that center around the needs of students and families in the surrounding neighborhood. For example, the development of after-school programs may alleviate parents' concerns over child care and provide opportunities for students to engage in enrichment activities. At one school, teachers proposed offering classes in areas that interested them. The school conducted a survey to identify potential courses to be taught and students who would be interested in taking them. Teachers had many skills and interests they could develop into after-school classes, including cooking, dancing, drafting, guitar playing, knitting, painting, photography, chess, scrapbooking, and sewing. Parents were encouraged to share their expertise as well. Teachers also recruited volunteers to coach basketball, soccer, and other sports students were interested in playing. Student involvement in extracurricular activities positively affected their academic performance, self-concept, and school climate (Fredricks & Eccles, 2006).

Teachers can also seek the help of existing organizations and programs whose initiatives are designed to promote student and family learning. Two programs to consider are Communities in School (CIS) and the 21st Century Community Learning Centers Program.

Communities in Schools is a nonprofit organization that helps schools identify the needs of their student population. After the needs have been identified, CIS serves as a link between teachers and the resources students need to stay in school and succeed academically. The work of CIS encompasses five basic principles:

- Strengthening students' relationships with adults through mentoring programs, tutoring services, and parental involvement programs
- Providing after-school activities and extended school hours
- Making health services such as counseling and assistance for teen parents accessible
- Developing students' work skills through the provision of technology workshops and other job-related activities
- Structuring service opportunities for students to give back to their community

The CIS website (http://www.communitiesinschools.org/) includes a link to success stories that you can use as a model to enhance the relationships you have already established with your community.

The 21st Century Community Learning Centers Program supports the creation of community learning centers and provides grant opportunities that teachers and administrators can pursue to develop academic enrichment opportunities for children and families in high-poverty schools. The after-school opportunities developed under this program must supplement regular academics and aim to increase student achievement in reading and math (Thompson & Winn Tutwiler, 2001). With support from these grants, for example, schools can fund personnel to teach adult basic literacy classes and English as a second language classes to the families of children in the school community. If you are interested in gathering additional information about the different kinds of after-school activities that can be provided at your school or want to learn more about promising practices in this area, consult the website of the National Center for Quality Afterschool at www.sedl.org/afterschool/.

Working with Community Organizations

Remember that community organizations may be able to provide a wide array of services to students and families in the school's neighborhood. Visit your local United Way website, which will retrieve a list of links to all of the nonprofit organizations found in your community. Many elementary schools are able to offer tutoring, mentoring, and after-school child care programs with the help of these organizations (as well as churches and colleges). As the following example suggests, children benefit from the services the organizations offer.

Orlando was a student in Mrs. Smith's bilingual kindergarten class. Because Mrs. Smith understood the importance of developing her students' native language to help them learn English, she engaged them in language development activities. However, she noticed that Orlando did not talk much. In fact, he imitated what the other children in class did. For instance, at the classroom learning centers, Orlando chose to point to objects that he wanted to play with or grabbed his classmates to show them what he wanted. To rule out that he had a hearing problem, Mrs. Smith reviewed the results of his health screening, which had been conducted at the beginning of the year. It indicated that Orlando's hearing was within normal range. Mrs. Smith had the school nurse rescreen Orlando's health and suggested to his parents that they take him to a mobile health clinic near the school. There, Orlando received a thorough medical examination. His parents learned that in addition to having a severe ear infection, Orlando had vision problems as well. He was referred to doctors who could provide him the medical attention and eye care he needed. His family also received information about programs that could provide medical assistance to low-income children.

Although mobile health clinics may not be available in every community, schools can look into partnering with local hospitals to provide free yearly check-ups to students' families. Teachers can also identify other school personnel who may be able to meet the needs of the school community. For example, the nurse at an elementary school organized health talks around allergies, nutrition, and other health topics that parents were interested in exploring.

Other services, such as individual and family counseling, can be attained by contacting institutions of higher learning that offer degree programs in these areas. University students majoring in psychology, education, counseling, social work, urban studies, and related areas often need practicum hours or internships. They might consider completing this requirement in a school setting.

As teachers work collaboratively with professionals in other disciplines, they may learn about different services available in the community. A directory of service agencies, organizations, programs, and other resources can then be put together for students and families to access when needed. A special education teacher, for example, compiled a list of agencies to which she had referred the families of students with disabilities. Included in the list were agencies responsible for providing services in the following categories:

- Adaptive equipment/assistive technology
- Advocacy services
- Adult day programs
- Early childhood intervention
- Financial planning
- Health care services
- Legal assistance
- Mental health supports
- Parent training programs
- Respite programs
- Support groups
- Transportation

You can generate a similar list for the community you serve. As a start, Figure 7.2 shows agencies that assist persons with special needs.

Creating Opportunities for Service Learning

Just as community organizations may provide a variety of resources to enrich the lives of those who live in the school neighborhood, students, families, and school personnel

FIGURE 7.2
Agencies That Help Persons with Special Needs

Adaptive Equipment/Assistive Technology

Able Data
http://www.abledata.com
Federally funded database with information on assistive technology and rehabilitation equipment for people with disabilities

Able People Foundation
http://www.ablepeoplefoundation.org
Nonprofit organization that assists people with disabilities to find and obtain mobility and assistive products to help them live independently

RehabTool
http://www.rehabtool.com
Provides free product search and referrals for assistive and adaptive technology (e.g., augmentative and alternative communication devices, computer access equipment, speech synthesis and voice recognition software) for people with physical disabilities

Advocacy Services/Legal Assistance

National Disability Rights Network
http://www.ndrn.org
Nonprofit organization that provides legal-based advocacy services to people with disabilities in the United States

ADA Watch
http://www.accessiblesociety.org/topics/ada/adawatchgroup.htm
Alliance of disability, civil rights, and social justice organizations committed to defending the rights of people with disabilities

Disability Rights Education and Defense Fund
http://www.dredf.org
Protects the civil rights of people with disabilities through legislation, litigation, and advocacy

Early Childhood Intervention

Easter Seals Child Development Centers
http://www.easterseals.com
Provides developmentally appropriate learning activities for children of all abilities

can contribute to strengthening these organizations and their communities when they engage in service learning opportunities. Service learning is a teaching strategy that connects what students learn in the classroom curriculum to the communities where they live (Wade, 1997). Following this approach, teachers (1) provide hands-on experiences for students to build academic skills in the context of doing community service and (2) build the time for students to reflect on how the service experience affects their ability to improve their community. Thus service learning teaches civic responsibility and develops students' ability to become problem solvers.

Teachers and students who engage in service learning projects can build positive relationships with the community by addressing community-identified needs. For example, Mrs. Hernandez's 3rd grade class developed a service learning project after a student raised questions about the number of homeless people in the surrounding neighborhood. Following this opportunity to teach her students about the causes of homelessness and its effects, Mrs. Hernandez had her students brainstorm ways to become involved in helping the homeless. With their teacher's guidance, students devoted time to conducting research about homelessness. They also wrote letters to community organizations dedicated to addressing the needs of the homeless and inquired about ways in which they could assist them. Students found they could donate food baskets to several shelters in the city. In preparation for making the baskets, the class learned about nutrition and made decisions about the best choices of food to include. Third grade representatives talked to the principal and PTA to start an event that helped collect the food. After the baskets had been assembled and distributed to the homeless shelter, the 3rd grade students shared their project at a school assembly and encouraged other students to undertake similar projects. Keep in mind that when parents participate in the various projects or when they accompany the class as chaperones, they benefit from the learning experience as well. See Figure 7.3 for some helpful websites and books associated with the implementation of service learning projects.

All stakeholders involved in children's education—parents, teachers, and students—need to take an active role in building relationships with the school community. The complexities that social, political, and economic factors impose on Latino families and their communities are multidimensional. If the goal is to provide a quality education to Latino children, school practitioners must acknowledge that they cannot meet this goal on their own. Reaching out to parents and communities should be a deliberate act, because at stake is the academic achievement of millions of Latino schoolchildren across the United States.

FIGURE 7.3
Service Learning Resources

Books

The Complete Guide to Service Learning: Proven, Practical Ways to Engage Students in Civic Responsibility, Academic Curriculum, and Social Action, by Catherine Berger Kaye (2004).

This book provides ideas for engaging students in service learning projects, as well as ways to connect service learning to different areas in the curriculum. Lists of literature that can be incorporated into various service learning ideas are provided.

The Kid's Guide to Service Projects: Over 500 Service Ideas for Young People Who Want to Make a Difference, by Barbara A. Lewis (1995).

Included here are ideas for how to engage young people in projects to help their community. Examples illustrate the difference that committed individuals—youth in particular—can make by getting involved in serving others.

Kids Taking Action: Community Service Learning Projects, K–8, by Pamela Roberts (2002).

This book presents 18 examples of community service learning projects in which K–8 teachers and students have participated, as well as ideas for hands-on activities that can be incorporated into these projects. An extended resource list and references on community service learning are also provided.

Websites

National Service Learning Clearinghouse

http://www.servicelearning.org

The Learn and Serve America's National Service Learning Clearinghouse provides comprehensive resources on service learning. In addition to examples of current service learning projects, the site offers lesson plans, bibliographies, and links to a library documenting the effectiveness of approaching learning through a service orientation.

Corporation for National and Community Service

http://www.learnandserve.gov

This website offers information about service learning for organizations or individuals interested in starting new projects. Links on the homepage retrieve examples of civic participation and volunteerism, as well as resources available to guide those interested in the integration of community service in the curricula.

National Service-Learning Partnership

http://www.service-learningpartnership.org

This website provides information about various foundations committed to solving social problems and opportunities available to take action throughout the United States. It publishes a newsletter and blog where people involved or interested in service learning can share ideas. Visitors to the website can access teaching resources for strengthening existing service learning programs and developing new ones.

TAKE **ACTION**

- Make a list of the assets found in the community where your school is located.
- Identify local businesses and organizations with which you could develop a partnership.
- Make a list of businesses in the community where you could take your students on a field trip.
- Identify community members (parents, business people, and others) who would be willing to share their areas of expertise with students in your school.
- Brainstorm ideas about how the interests of your students, students' families, and colleagues could be developed into an after-school class.
- Contact local universities or other learning institutions to inquire about how you could work together to meet your students' needs.
- Familiarize yourself with service learning and seek opportunities to integrate it into your teaching.

8

Designing Campuswide Plans for Parental Engagement

As we noted in Chapter 7, schools cannot reach all their goals alone. In any community, schools need parental support to sustain the academic progress of students, and engaging parents can have positive effects on classrooms, the school campus, and the community at large. Initiatives for increasing Latino parental engagement involve innovation and change—change that must begin at the level of the individual, as described in Chapter 1. Chapter 1 also outlined how change begins with understanding one's own perceptions about Latino parents and by identifying influencing factors. In this chapter, we offer additional suggestions for how to identify and understand perceptions about Latino parents on your campus and how to form a campus task force to increase parental engagement, and we present ideas for framing campus goals and objectives that align with this initiative. We begin, however, with information related to civil rights, because knowing about students' rights in U.S. schools provides the context for and is a crucial step in framing goals associated with increasing parental involvement.

Civil Rights of Students

Although most of the federal policies described in the following abbreviated list were enacted more than 30 years ago, some individuals on your campus, as well as parents of language-minority students, may lack this information. These policies were enacted through our legal system to preserve justice and ensure that civil rights are protected for students enrolled in U.S. schools, including those who may speak a language other than English.

Title VI of the Civil Rights Act of 1964

Title VI prohibits discrimination on the grounds of race, color, or national origin by recipients of federal financial assistance. The Title VI regulatory requirements have been interpreted by the court system to prohibit denial of equal access to education because of a language-minority student's limited proficiency in English.

Lau v. Nichols

This 1974 Supreme Court case involved parents who petitioned against the failure of the San Francisco Unified School District to provide English language instruction to approximately 1,800 students of Chinese heritage who did not speak English. The schools they attended had provided inadequate instructional programs, thereby denying students a meaningful opportunity to participate in the public educational program. The Supreme Court found a violation of the equal education opportunities provision of the Civil Rights Act of 1964. In his opinion outlining implementation regulations for the Department of Health, Education, and Welfare, Justice William O. Douglas (as cited in García, 2009) wrote the following:

> Basic English skills are at the very core of what these public schools teach. Imposition of a requirement that, before a child can effectively participate in the educational program, he must already have acquired those basic skills is to make a mockery of public education. We know that those who do not understand English are certain to find their classroom experiences wholly incomprehensible and in no way meaningful. (p. 170)

Another important law was established by the Fifth Circuit Court through the ruling of *Castañeda vs. Pickard* (1981). The court ruled that schools must take "appropriate action" regarding students learning English and that such action must be based on sound educational theory, produce results, and provide adequate resources, teachers, and materials (García, 2009).

Equal Educational Opportunities Act of 1974

This civil rights statute prohibits states from denying equal educational opportunity to an individual on account of "race, color, sex, or national origin" and specifically by "the failure of an educational agency to take appropriate action to overcome language barriers that impede equal participation by its students in its instructional programs."

ASPIRA v. New York City Board of Education

The Puerto Rican Legal Defense and Education Fund filed its first lawsuit in 1972, *ASPIRA v. New York City Board of Education*, a case that resulted in the groundbreaking ASPIRA Consent Decree (ASPIRA is a nonprofit organization dedicated to developing the educational and leadership capacity of Hispanic youth). The decree forced the city's school system to implement bilingual education techniques as a way to provide effective instruction for non-English-speaking students.

Plyler v. Doe

In 1982, the Supreme Court ruled in *Plyler v. Doe* that public schools were prohibited from denying immigrant students access to a public education, stating that undocumented children have the same right to a free public education as U.S. citizens and permanent residents. Undocumented immigrant students are obligated, as are all other students, to attend school until they reach the age mandated by state law.

Immigration Enforcement Measures

An important matter that bears heavily on Latino students who are undocumented citizens are "sweeps" by Immigration and Customs Enforcement (ICE), a branch of the U.S. Department of Homeland Security. The sweeps are occasions when ICE agents raid places where they suspect there are undocumented persons, arrest them, and arrange for their deportation. Some of these sweeps occur in workplaces and involve parents whose children are at school at the time. Imagine the horror that children experience when they return to an empty home only to learn that their family members have been detained by immigration officials. Because children often consider school to be their second home, many of them immediately run in panic to their classroom and their teacher. In other instances, the children who have been part of an immigration sweep have lived in cells (once designated as prison cells) with their mothers, which violates minimum standards and conditions for the housing and release of all minors in federal immigration custody.

Teachers, together with their campus leadership team, should be familiar with the national, state, and local policies that establish schools as "safe zones." In a "safe zone," subpoenas and other judicial writs must be obtained and presented before any student information can be released to individuals not authorized by schools or their school district. Specifically, the Family Educational Rights and Privacy Act prohibits any outside agency, including Immigration and Customs Enforcement, from obtaining student information without parental permission or a valid court order. In short, school personnel are under no mandate to disclose to federal, state, or local government officials whether or not a student (and the student's family) is documented.

The DREAM Act

Many immigrant Latino students are thriving in their current educational settings as afforded by law, and some continue to qualify for and gain admission to college. Because these young people could never travel to and from their family's country of origin, part of their bicultural identity encompasses those elements from U.S. mainstream culture they have made their own—including school.

However, many undocumented youth find it challenging to continue their schooling in higher education. Under current immigration regulations, children who immigrate to the United States from another country can obtain permanent status only through their parents and may not independently apply for legal residency. The process inevitably involves complications, making each petition unique. Children have the right to attend and complete K–12 public education, but upon graduation, they are not allowed to attend college in many states. In the states where they may do so, they are not eligible to apply for financial aid, they cannot be hired for a work-study job, and they are required to pay international tuition rates. Without proof of legal residency status, these youths are generally not issued driver's licenses or Social Security cards. This means that they cannot be hired to work even if they earn an advanced degree.

The Development, Relief and Education for Alien Minors Act (the "DREAM Act") was introduced in the U.S. Congress in 2009. Though the bill passed in the House of Representatives, it was later blocked in the Senate, despite hunger strikes, sit-ins, and vibrant organized marches and rallies in support of the bill. This bill proposed to provide immigrant youth who graduated from a U.S. high school the opportunity to gain residency status (i.e., a "Green Card"). The legislation would have provided immigration benefits to those who arrived in the United States before age 16 and who have been living in the United States continuously for at least five years before the enactment of the act. Under the act, immigrant students would have qualified, in part, by meeting the following additional requirements:

- Must be between the ages of 12 and 35 at the time the law is enacted.
- Must have graduated from a U.S. high school or obtained a General Education Diploma.
- Must have "good moral character."

In addition to qualifying for legal residency status, immigrant students would have also been entitled to apply for student loans and work-study at institutions of higher education but would have remained ineligible to apply for Pell educational grants. (For additional information, go to http://www.dreamact2009.org/.)

Forming a Task Force

When considering how to increase Latino parents' engagement at school and planning for campuswide change, identifying key individuals who can lead and organize the effort becomes instrumental. The individuals—who should all have a high interest in improving Latino parental engagement—can make up a task force charged with achieving this goal.

One of the task force's first objectives should be to assess the existing campuswide perceptions of the Latino families they serve. Some initial questions to consider include the following:

- Do we know how students, teachers, administrators, and support staff perceive Latino parental involvement on our campus?
- How do parental-involvement initiatives at the district level affect Latino parental involvement on our campus?
- What procedure can we use to examine perceptions about Latino parental involvement at a campus level?

Figure 8.1 provides additional questions to consider in assessing the perceptions of campus personnel.

Any procedure for assessing perceptions should be based on the needs of the school community, be aligned with administrative protocols, and be documented so that progress can be measured. One way to begin implementing a process for collecting information may be to have the task force assemble a team of school personnel to identify the perceptions the stakeholders have. A team leader (a teacher or a member of the campus leadership team) can be assigned responsibility for coordinating the project. This person's primary responsibility is to manage, track, and facilitate the collection of information while ensuring that mutual respect and confidentiality are maintained throughout the process.

FIGURE 8.1
Questions for Assessing Staff Views on Parental Involvement

- Why should Latino parental involvement be improved?
- What are some desired outcomes?
- What aspects of parental involvement seem to be working now?
- What barriers are there?
- Who on campus might be interested in increasing Latino parental involvement?
- What parts of the school organization would be involved in improving Latino parental involvement?
- What functions of the school organization would be affected?

The team leader should recruit team members (with the number determined by the scope of established goals, objectives, and activities) and determine the procedures for collecting information. Additionally, the team leader determines how to analyze the information collected and verify that the interpretation of the information is accurate. Last, the team leader generates a plan for aligning the collected information with the goals, objectives, and activities established by the team. It is important to have a lead organizer so that the team has momentum in advancing toward set goals and objectives. However, due to the scope of professional responsibilities, we recommend ensuring that the team leader, campus administrators, and team members all have close working relationships.

Once the team is formed, all its decision-making activities should take place during scheduled meetings. One of its first tasks will be to identify the groups (parents, teachers, and others) from which to solicit information. The members may decide to collect data from each group at different times, or they may decide to assign team members to collect information from designated groups simultaneously, through a coordinated effort. In any case, it is important to establish guiding principles for executing the process and to delineate goals and outcomes. Regular meetings also offer time to establish procedures for scheduling additional meetings and for determining objectives, activities, and time lines. In sum, the team works collaboratively to design criteria that will enable them to evaluate the information-gathering process by tracking and measuring progress in meeting the goals and outcomes they have established.

The procedures used to collect information should be clearly outlined and documented. This information should be carefully maintained and organized so that it can be shared at any time with teachers, parents, administrators, and other individuals with a relevant interest. It is also especially important that those interviewed be informed about (1) who will have access to the information they provide, (2) how anonymity will be preserved, (3) how the information collected will be safeguarded, and (4) what will happen with the information once the process of collecting it is complete. Persons who know that their responses will be safeguarded and anonymous are more likely to participate in the process. Participants can be asked questions such as those outlined in Figure 8.1 or asked these two primary questions:

- How can we improve parental involvement?
- How can parents support the academic progress of their children?

Groups to be interviewed may include Latino parents, students, teachers, and other school workers, such as paraeducators, administrative assistants, counselors, custodians, and cafeteria staff. The process should take into account campus needs and follow the administrative protocol at all times, with guiding principles that reflect mutual respect and confidentiality for all participants.

An important consideration concerns the manner in which responses are given. That is, whereas teachers may respond through written forms, parents will benefit from being offered a variety of response modes. Some may feel more comfortable responding to questions orally, and others may choose to respond in writing; and the majority may be able to participate only if they can use Spanish to express their ideas. Simply stated, the process of collecting information from parents must include knowledgeable individuals who speak Spanish and English, who are familiar with the community that the school serves, and who also have an interest in improving Latino parental involvement.

After the team collects, reads, and categorizes the information, the members can meet to share their findings, which are now data (see Figure 8.2 for instructions on how to evaluate the collected data). The goal of this meeting is to find commonalities and differences in how the information was interpreted and to gain through discussion an understanding of any remarks that may seem ambiguous or unclear. This process may take one or several meetings, and it may require inviting a translator or other individuals who may contribute to generating reliable interpretation of the information.

In their analysis of what parents, teachers, students, and others think, the team members may decide to identify the themes and patterns emerging from the responses and then organize this information into categories they have designed. After the team has thoroughly analyzed and discussed the data, they can hold separate meetings with parents, teachers, and students (if age-appropriate). At each meeting, team members can restate the goals, objectives, and procedures of the information-gathering process and share the findings from the responses. These meetings enable the team to verify that their interpretations of the information were accurate. The feedback provided at each meeting is then noted and used to revise or clarify aspects of the information already analyzed.

FIGURE 8.2
Process for Evaluating Data on Perceptions of Latino Parental Involvement

The team leader—

- Recruits three team members to ensure broad interpretation of the data (i.e., the responses).
- Duplicates data to generate a copy for each team member.
- Asks team members to read the data.
- Schedules meetings to monitor progress, answer questions, reestablish guiding principles of respect and confidentiality.

To evaluate the data, team members—

- Separate the data into categories according to respondents (parents, teachers, others).
- Further categorize the responses as follows:
  - Remarks that appear frequently (e.g., "I never know where to park on campus," "I never know when I can park in front of the school")
  - Remarks that offer solutions (e.g., "Let's put orange cones out to show where parking is not allowed," "Can we paint a crosswalk?")
  - Remarks that are barriers (e.g., "I can't see why I can't park in front of the school when I've seen other parents do it," "Nobody cares about other people's children; they only care for the safety of their own")
  - Remarks that are novel and interesting (e.g., "All the other elementary schools in the district have employees guiding the children at dismissal," "My cousin is a police officer and can help us get organized")

The primary goal of the team members is to ensure that they have reliably interpreted the data. After attaining this goal, the team members meet again to identify with more certainty the existing assets and barriers with regard to parental involvement. Using the information they've collected, they can then proceed to align the goals, objectives, and activities to strengthen involvement, which are important steps in forming a systematic plan to strengthen home-to-school partnerships.

Indeed, identifying the perceptions that campus personnel have of Latino parents can be useful in improving parental involvement. Consider the qualitative study of Quiocho and Daoud (2006), who examined issues of perception regarding Latino parental involvement. They studied the current level of Latino parental involvement and also identified factors that influenced an increase in Latino parental participation. Part of their investigation included interviewing teachers at two schools serving large Mexican American student populations. The teachers were asked, "How can we improve parental involvement?" Here are some of their responses:

- "They [parents] don't and can't help in the classroom."
- "They are illiterate."
- "They don't help their children with homework."
- "They take their children to Mexico for almost anything throughout the year and keep them away from school for weeks. How can the children learn this way?"
- "They just don't care as much as other parents do." (p. 260)

The next question asked, "How can parents support the academic progress of their children?" Here are some of the teachers' responses:

- "Parents can't help with the homework."
- "Parents don't speak English, so how can they help?"
- "Kids leave for vacations and they don't do any work we assign when they are gone."
- "Children don't work as hard as other students."
- "Children start from a different place in literacy." (p. 260)

Quiocho and Daoud conclude that some teachers held a deficit view of Latino parents' ability to sustain a home-to-school partnership and a belief that parents had limited abilities to support their children's academic progress.

When the researchers posed the same initial question to Latino parents ("How can we improve parental involvement?"), some of the responses included the following:

- "Improve communication between teachers and parents."
- "Offer workshops that help parents understand children's school work (and assignments)."
- "Make sure that parents understand the work children are assigned (at home and at school)."
- "Schedule conferences with parents every two months."

- "Personally invite parents [to come to school activities or to conferences] through phone calls."

The researchers also asked parents, "What obstacles exist that you believe affect the academic achievement of your children?" The researchers report the following:

- Parents did not want their children to ask for help and then receive no response from teachers.
- Parents wanted access to the core curriculum and wanted the singing, the drawing, and television watching at school to stop. [English-speaking students in other classrooms were receiving content instruction.]
- Parents wanted access to books in Spanish so they could help their children understand school assignments taught in English only.
- Parents wanted teachers to be friendlier, to respect their children, and to keep promises made to the students (for example, in regard to field trips). (pp. 261–262)

After administering their interview protocols and analyzing the data, Quiocho and Daoud facilitated the sharing of information across groups (parents and teachers). Thereafter, the researchers facilitated ongoing meetings between both groups, enabling parents and teachers to continue to discuss the topics that emerged from the data. The results of these exchanges fostered reciprocity in the sharing of ideas and inspired mutual learning. Through reciprocal sharing of ideas and aiming for mutual understanding, parents and teachers were able to establish working relationships based on mutual interests in strengthening home-to-school partnerships.

Organizing the Campus

Once campus perceptions of Latino parental engagement have been assessed and analyzed, the next step is to assess the organization of your school campus. Generally, campus administrators are most knowledgeable about the functions, organization, and policies that govern a campus. Therefore, the parental-involvement task force will need to rely on campus administrators to determine how the goals, objectives, and activities are aligned with campus procedures and protocols.

Understanding how the campus functions and is organized enables the task force to make decisions about how to structure a plan to increase Latino parental involvement. You can use Reproducible A.20a to organize the plan. With the guidance of campus administrators, the task force assesses levels of change for each initiative. In the example provided in Reproducible A.20b, the team chose to assess the task of strengthening parental involvement in the PTA. The assigned team recorder identified the parents, the PTA, teacher leaders, administrators, and the campus instructional coordinator as the subgroups responsible for the task, noting the responsibilities of each subgroup. At the initial meeting, the level of expected change was documented as "initiating" or "ongoing." When the team met, observations were recorded so that progress could be assessed. In some instances, the level of change progressed from "initiating" to "intermediate," while in other instances, it remained at "ongoing."

Reproducible A.20a can be used to monitor a variety of issues and tasks, including parental understanding of grade-level standards and benchmarks, informal assessments, school routines and policies, school celebrations, and reading initiatives. The form enables the team to document and celebrate change, provide evidence of benefits gained, and increase participation across all subgroups. In sum, by understanding the functions of the organization, the task force can also set objectives, outline and delegate tasks to group members, establish time lines, and generate criteria by which to measure their progress. Working collaboratively, the team can facilitate enacting a plan once it is structured.

An important element of implementing change to increase Latino parental engagement is to identify how to work within the organization and functions of your campus. This effort increases the opportunities for implementing innovative ideas and actions that are generated. The underlying implication is that documentation is fundamental to tracking progress and useful for setting future goals. The documentation of practices and procedures also helps to establish criteria by which to evaluate outcomes.

Deciding on Campus Goals and Action Plans

The parental-involvement task force should also analyze the different models of parental involvement and their outcomes (Olivos, 2006). Campuswide decisions about outcomes should guide the campus plan that the team designs. For example, the task force may consider the following questions to guide the development of campus goals and outcomes. Is the goal to have Latino parents—

- Learn the behaviors and values of the school?
- Practice the behaviors and values of the school?

- Participate in posing problems and seeking solutions and also have a voice in decision making?
- Become agents of change, using their rights to voice their own needs, contribute solutions, pose their own problems, and seek representation in decision making?

Considering the busy context in which schools operate, the plan generated by the task force must be incremental (executed over time), be practical, be manageable, and engage school practitioners. The campus plan must also incorporate shifts in demographics and needs, which include cultural and linguistic diversity. For example, many Latino parents speak only Spanish, but others may speak English as a second language with varying levels of proficiency. An action plan may also include the following components:

- *Seeking grants to sponsor seminars aligned with the interests of Latino parents.*
- *Ensuring that all parent meetings are inclusive.* This may require having a translator, organizing breakout sessions based on parents' language preference, or having a translator for Spanish-speaking parents, who wear wireless earphones.
- *Coordinating and documenting all community outreach efforts as part of the campus improvement plan or school district reports* (Reproducible A.21 can help track parental involvement for the fall/spring semesters). For example, a designated person charged with coordinating the Latino parental-involvement initiative can keep activity calendars and display them in a prominent place on campus for parents and school practitioners to see. Also, documentation from sign-in sheets from each meeting with parents can be added to the information included in a monthly campus report.
- *Using Title I funding to add a social worker to the staff.* This individual would work in coordination with the school counselor to offer additional support to children and their families, who may live in high-poverty zones or have other social needs.
- *Ensuring that professional school practitioners can translate for parents.* Parents have the right to receive accurate and complete information regarding assessment outcomes and how screening processes affect student placement. For example, certified bilingual education teachers, who have received training on procedures and terminology, can translate and facilitate the Admission, Review, and Dismissal process involved in a student's placement in special education. Translators are also needed to provide information about language support

programs, standardized testing and the implications linked to outcomes, and other educational programs.

- *Hiring certified language support teachers and specialists whose credentials are aligned with the academic needs of linguistically and culturally diverse student populations.* These teachers can offer English language learners an asset-based approach to instruction by fortifying and advancing each student's current knowledge and abilities. Teacher-specialists can also more precisely share data with parents about student progress and achievement, which is associated with providing equity in educational opportunities.

The task force should also assume the responsibility for reconciling differing perspectives and gaining the cooperation of all school practitioners. The task force members can serve as ambassadors or liaisons, documenting and communicating their assigned duties to their colleagues on campus as they design campus goals through collaborative efforts.

Clearing Up Expectations

The goal of extending equity in educational opportunities to English language learners through the enhanced engagement of their parents must be clearly communicated to campus personnel. When teachers and administrators believe that increasing Latino parental involvement is a priority, then a campus action plan must follow. Structuring, managing, organizing, and sustaining a systematic plan will require that all tasks and activities are aligned with this goal. Additionally, all stakeholders must be informed and have opportunities to participate. Within a home-to-school partnership, this means that information must flow in both directions to ensure inclusivity. Therefore, all stakeholders must understand why increasing Latino parental involvement matters, what elements of change may occur, which functions of the school organization will be affected (how and why), which facets of the organization will be involved, and how their own roles will be instrumental in implementing a campuswide plan to increase Latino parental engagement.

Each step taken to implement a campuswide plan offers teachers, administrators, and others on campus opportunities to inform, to invite, to discuss, and to learn with different stakeholders who have varying interests and roles. Thus any plan can offer utility as well as flexibility and creativity. These attributes are essential when planning for campuswide needs and those associated with a particular community.

Ultimately, increasing Latino parental involvement begins with valuing home-to-school partnerships. It is sustained by identifying needs and aspirations, by individual effort, by a commitment to securing the rights of parents and their children to access to the academic curriculum, and by making clear the expectations regarding the indispensable role of Latino parents as partners in the school community.

TAKE **ACTION**

- Research students' educational and civil rights under federal mandates affecting English language learners.
- Become knowledgeable about the policies that govern equity in schooling for all students in your state as well as on a national level.
- Assess campus personnel's perceptions about Latino parental involvement before attempting to implement changes.
- Identify how community organizations can support your campaign for increasing Latino parental involvement at school.
- Identify national, state, and local policies that govern and organizations that advocate for Latino parental and student rights.

Afterword

Latino families today, whether they have just immigrated to the United States or are removed generationally from this experience, understand the value of an education in a global society. Latino parents understand that an education may be the only way to improve the economic prospects for their children, and seeking an improved livelihood was a compelling reason for leaving their country of origin. Latino parents also recognize that to negotiate their own social integration in U.S. society and broker the same for their children, they must understand how schooling functions, understand the authority that schools wield, and manage the ways in which schooling affects their children.

Teachers and school leadership teams understand that they cannot accomplish their goals in isolation, removed from the community they serve. Campus leaders recognize that to attain the academic advancement of Latino students, they must listen to and engage parents' voiced needs concerning the educational aspirations they hold for their children. School leaders are responsible for enacting authentic partnership models that include students, parents, and key stakeholders within the community.

We collaborated to write this text to assemble the ideas that stemmed from our own teaching experiences, our fieldwork with teachers and administrators, and research-based findings associated with teaching Latino students. We have aimed to generate concrete and practical applications, sharing ideas and activities grounded in the goal of increasing Latino parental engagement. Although the complexities involved in working with any community are greater than what a text can address, we hope that the information that we share may spark discussions with colleagues and inspire continued exploration of the issues that affect the education of English learners.

APPENDIX A

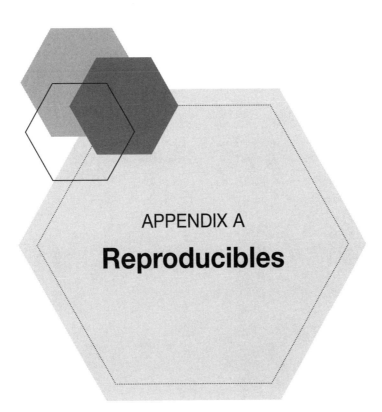

Reproducibles

Reproducible A.1: Helpful Spanish Words and Phrases

Pronouns	***Pronombres Personales***
I	*yo*
me	*mí*
my	*mi*
mine	*mío*
you (singular)/you (plural)	*tú/ustedes*
your (singular)/your (plural)	*su/su*
he	*él*
his	*su*
she	*ella*
her	*su*
it	*eso*
we	*nosotros/nosotras*
our	*nuestro*
they	*ellos/ellas*
their	*su*

Verbs	***Verbos***
circle	*dibujar un círculo*
color	*colorear*
come	*venir*
cut	*cortar*
draw	*dibujar*
enter	*entrar*
finish/complete	*terminar/completar*
follow	*seguir*
get	*agarrar*
give	*dar*
glue	*pegar*
go	*ir*
hand	*dar*

Reproducible A.1: Helpful Spanish Words and Phrases (*continued*)

Verbs	*Verbos*
handwrite	*escribir a mano*
line up	*ponerse en línea*
listen	*escuchar*
place	*poner*
print	*imprimir*
read	*leer*
sit	*sentarse*
stand	*pararse*
stop	*parar/detenerse*
study	*estudiar*
talk/discuss	*hablar/discutir*
turn over	*voltear*
underline	*subrayar*
walk	*caminar*
write	*escribir*

Classroom Nouns	*Objetos Alrededor del Salón de Clase*
assignment/homework	*asignatura/tarea*
book	*libro*
chair	*silla*
chalk	*gis/tiza*
chalkboard	*pizarrón*
classroom	*salón de clases*
closet	*clóset/armario*
coat hanger	*lugar para colgar los abrigos*
computer	*computador/computadora*
crayon	*crayón/color*
cubby	*estante*
desk	*escritorio*

Reproducible A.1: Helpful Spanish Words and Phrases (*continued*)

Classroom Nouns	*Objetos Alrededor del Salón de Clase*
door	*puerta*
dry-erase board	*pizarra*
file cabinet	*archivero*
glue	*goma/pegamento*
marker	*marcador*
math	*matemáticas*
paper	*papel*
paper clip	*clip/sujetador de papeles*
pen	*pluma/bolígrafo*
pencil	*lápiz*
poster	*póster*
reading	*lectura*
restroom	*baño*
rug	*alfombra/tapete/carpeta*
scissors	*tijeras*
shelf	*estante*
sign	*anuncio/señalamiento*
social studies	*estudios sociales/ciencias sociales*
spelling	*deletreo*
stapler	*grapadora*
tack	*tachuela*
tape	*cinta adhesiva*
wall	*pared*
water fountain	*bebedero*
whiteboard	*pizarra blanca*
window	*ventana*
word wall	*pared de palabras*
worksheet	*hoja de trabajo*
writing	*escritura*

Reproducible A.1: Helpful Spanish Words and Phrases (*continued*)

Classroom Rules	***Reglas del Salón de Clase***
Be kind to others.	*Sé amable con los demás.*
Be polite and courteous.	*Sé educado y cortés.*
Be prepared to learn.	*Está preparado para aprender.*
Complete your assignments.	*Completa/termina tu trabajo/tarea.*
Follow directions.	*Sigue instrucciones.*
Keep hands, objects, and feet to yourself.	*Mantén manos, pies, y objetos cerca de tí.*
Listen quietly.	*Escucha con atención.*
Make good choices.	*Toma buenas decisiones.*
Raise your hand if you have a question.	*Levanta la mano si tienes una pregunta.*
Respect others.	*Respeta a los demás.*
Share.	*Comparte.*
Stay on task.	*Mantente enfocado.*
Use an inside voice.	*Usa tu voz baja.*
Walk in the building.	*Camina en el edificio.*

Motivating Phrases	***Frases para Motivar***
Be courageous!	*¡Sé valiente!*
Be positive!	*¡Sé positivo!*
Believe in yourself.	*Cree en tí mismo.*
Challenge yourself.	*Ponte retos.*
Do your best.	*Haz lo mejor que puedas.*
Explore the world.	*Explora el mundo.*
Hang in there.	*Mantente ahí.*
If at first you don't succeed, try, try again.	*Si no tienes éxito la primera vez, trata una y otra vez.*
Never give up.	*Nunca te des por vencido.*
Never stop learning.	*Nunca dejes de aprender.*
Persevere.	*Persevera.*
Read.	*Lee.*
Try your hardest.	*Trata de hacer lo mejor que puedas.*

Reproducible A.1: Helpful Spanish Words and Phrases (*continued*)

Motivating Phrases	*Frases para Motivar*
Winners never quit, and quitters never win.	*Los ganadores nunca se dan por vencidos y quienes se dan por vencidos, nunca ganan.*
Yes, you can!	*¡Sí, tú puedes!*
You can do it!	*¡Tú puedes hacerlo!*

Pillars of Character Education	*Pilares del Buen Carácter*
caring	*que se preocupa por los demás*
citizenship	*ciudadanía*
courage	*valor*
diligence	*diligencia*
fairness/justice	*justicia*
honesty	*honestidad*
integrity	*integridad*
respect	*respeto*
responsibility	*responsabilidad*
trustworthiness	*alguien digno de confianza*

Cafeteria	*Cafetería*
cafeteria	*cafetería*
chocolate milk	*leche de chocolate*
cup	*taza*
dish	*plato*
drink (n.), drink (v.)	*bebida, beber*
eat	*comer*
fork	*tenedor*
knife	*cuchillo*
line, line up	*línea, ponerse en línea*
milk	*leche*
napkin	*servilleta*
pay	*pagar*

Reproducible A.1: Helpful Spanish Words and Phrases (*continued*)

Cafeteria	*Cafetería*
plate	*plato*
spoon	*cuchara*
table	*mesa*
tray	*charola*
water	*agua*

Library	*Biblioteca*
books	*libros*
card	*tarjeta*
check out	*sacar libros*
due	*fecha de regreso*
librarian	*bibliotecario(a)*
library	*biblioteca*
shelves	*estantes/repisas*
sign (your name)	*firma (tu nombre)*

General	*General*
Bless you	*Salud*
Bye	*Adiós*
Don't worry	*No te preocupes*
Excuse me	*Con permiso*
Good afternoon	*Buenas tardes*
Good idea	*Buena idea*
Good morning	*Buenos días*
Happy birthday	*Feliz cumpleaños*
Hello. How are you?	*Hola. ¿Cómo estás?*
Nice to meet you	*Mucho gusto*
No	*No*
Please	*Por favor*
Thank you	*Gracias*

Reproducible A.1: Helpful Spanish Words and Phrases (*continued*)

General	***General***
Very good	*Muy bien*
Wow	*Guau*
Yes	*Sí*

Reproducible A.2a: Sample Introductory Letter to Parents

Dear ______________________________:

Welcome to our school community! I am so happy to be your child's teacher. I can already tell that ______________________________ is going to be a wonderful addition to our classroom. Because I want the very best for your child, I want to work with you. I want your child to succeed at school, so whenever you have any questions or concerns, please do not hesitate to contact me at ______________________________. Or feel free to drop by at ______________________________. Our school has a Spanish-speaking interpreter whose name is ______________________________ and who can be contacted at ______________________________ if you need help communicating information to me. What is the best way to contact you?

I also want to invite you to meet with me so that I can show you our classroom and give you a tour of our campus. I would love for you to meet some of our teachers and administrators. This would give me the opportunity to ask you some questions about your child. I value your input.

I cannot wait to meet you.

Your child's teacher,

- -

Yes, I want to meet with you. I can meet on ______________ at ______________.

The best way to contact me is: ______________ home number

______________ cell number

______________ e-mail address

Reproducible A.2b: Ejemplo de una Carta de Presentación para los Padres de Niños Latinos que Aprenden Inglés

Estimado(a) ______________________________:

¡Bienvenido a la comunidad de nuestra escuela! Estoy muy contento(a) de ser el/la maestro(a) de su niño(a). Estoy seguro(a) que ______________________________ va a ser una excelente adición a nuestro salón de clases. Porque quiero lo mejor para su hijo(a), quiero trabajar con usted. Quiero que su niño(a) tenga éxito en la escuela. Por eso, cuando tenga cualquier pregunta o preocupación, no dude en comunicarse conmigo al ______________________________. O siéntase con la libertad de buscarme en ______________________________. Nuestra escuela tiene un(a) intérprete que habla español. Su nombre es ______________________________ y puede comunicarse con él/ella al ______________________________ si necesita ayuda para darme cualquier información. ¿Cuál es la mejor manera en la que yo puedo comunicarme con usted?

También quiero invitarlo a que me conozca para enseñarle nuestro salón y darle un paseo por nuestra escuela. Me gustaría que conociera a algunos de nuestros maestros y directores. Esto me daría la oportunidad de hacerle algunas preguntas acerca de su niño(a). Valoro la información que usted pueda compartir conmigo.

Espero conocerlo(a) pronto.

El/la maestro(a) de su niño(a),

- -

Sí, quiero reunirme con usted. Podemos reunirnos el ________________ a las ________________.

Puede comunicarse conmigo al: ______________ número de casa
______________ número de celular
______________ dirección de correo electrónico.

Reproducible A.3a: Letter to Parents About Specific Websites

Dear Parent:

I noticed that—

☐ Your child has expressed an interest in ______________________.
If you have the opportunity, please visit this website with your child:
______________________.

You will notice that there are many wonderful pictures and interesting information that I know you and your child will appreciate.

☐ Your child has had difficulty with ______________________.
If you have the opportunity, please visit this website with your child:
______________________.

You will notice that there are many opportunities for your child to practice and refine his/her skills.

☐ There is a wonderful website filled with many ideas for how to help your child with ______________________. If you have the opportunity, please visit this website with your child: ______________________.

I'm sure that you will find these beneficial.
If you have difficulty accessing the website, please let me know.

With appreciation,

Your child's teacher

Reproducible A.3b:
Carta a los Padres Aacerca de Sitios Específicos de Internet

Estimado(a) padre/madre:

Me he dado cuenta de que:

☐ Su hijo(a) ha expresado un interés en ________________________.
Si tiene oportunidad, por favor visite este sitio de Internet con su niño(a): ________________________.

Se dará cuenta de que tiene fotografías maravillosas e información interesante que sé que usted y su hijo(a) apreciarán.

☐ Su hijo(a) ha tenido dificultad con ________________________.
Si tiene oportunidad, por favor visite este sitio de Internet con su niño(a): ________________________.

Se dará cuenta de que hay muchas oportunidades para que su hijo(a) practique o refine sus destrezas.

☐ Hay un sitio de Internet con muchas ideas de cómo usted puede ayudar a su hijo(a) con: ________________________. Si tiene oportunidad, por favor visite este sitio de Internet con su hijo(a): ________________________.

Estoy seguro(a) de que estos sitios de internet le serán útiles.

Si tiene dificultad para entrar al sitio de Internet, por favor avíseme.

El/la maestro(a) de su hijo(a)

Reproducible A.4: Home Visit Record

Date: ______________________ Time: ______________________

Child's name: ____

Parent's name: ____

What was the purpose of the home visit?

Was the purpose of the home visit accomplished? Why? Why not?

What recommendations were made by the parents or the teacher?

What did I learn from this home visit?

Where do I go from here?

Reproducible A.5a: Home Language Survey

Home Language Survey
[School District]
[School Year]

Date: ______________________

Student's last name: ____________ First: ____________ Middle: ____________

Gender: ____ Male ____ Female Grade level: ____________

Date of birth: ____________________ Place of birth: ____________________

Parent's/guardian's name: ______________________________________

Parent's/guardian's address: ______________________________________

Parent's/guardian's phone number(s): ______________________________

What is/was the student's first language? __________________________

Does the student speak a language(s) other than English? _____ Yes _____ No
If yes, specify: ____

What language is spoken most often by the student? ______________________

What language is spoken most often at home? __________________________

What language is spoken most often by the adults in the home? ______________

How many years did the child attend a school outside the United States? ________

When did the child first attend a school in the United States? ______________

Person completing this form: ______________________________________

Parent/guardian signature: ____________________ Date: ________________

Reproducible A.5b: Cuestionario del Lenguaje en el Hogar

Cuestionario del Lenguaje en el Hogar
[Distrito Escolar]
[Año Escolar]

Fecha: ______________________

Apellido: __________ Nombre: __________ Segundo nombre: __________

Género: ____ Masculino ____ Femenino Grado/año escolar: __________

Fecha de nacimiento: __________ Lugar de nacimiento: __________

Nombre del padre/madre/guardián legal: ______________________

Dirección del padre/madre/guardián legal: ______________________

Número(s) de teléfono del padre/madre/guardián legal: ______________

¿Cuál es/fue el primer lenguaje del estudiante? ______________________

¿Habla el estudiante un lenguaje(s) que no sea el inglés? _____ Sí _____ No
Si sí, especifíque: ______________________

¿Cuál es el lenguaje que más habla el estudiante? ______________________

¿Cuál es el lenguaje que más se habla en casa? ______________________

¿Cuál es el lenguaje que más hablan los adultos en casa? ______________

¿Cuántos años estuvo el niño(a) en una escuela fuera de los Estados Unidos? ______

¿Cuándo vino por primera vez el niño(a) a una escuela en los Estados Unidos? _____

Nombre de la persona que completa esta forma: ______________________

Firma del padre/madre/guardián: ______________ Fecha: __________

Reproducible A.6a: Template for Learning Vocabulary

Write the vocabulary word in English, and then illustrate it and write its translation and definition in Spanish. Fold this paper into a third to cover your illustration and Spanish translation. Keep this folded over to study the word in English, and open the fold whenever you need help remembering its definition.

English	Illustration	Spanish

English	Illustration	Spanish

English	Illustration	Spanish

English	Illustration	Spanish

English	Illustration	Spanish

Reproducible A.6b:
Modelo para el Aprendizaje de Palabras de Vocabulario

Escribe las palabras de vocabulario en inglés, ilústralas y escribe su traducción al español. Dobla este papel en tres partes para cubrir tu dibujo y la palabra en español y escribe la definición en el cuadro. Mantén el papel doblado para estudiar la palabra y ábrelo cuando necesites ayuda para recordar la definición.

Inglés	Ilustración/dibujo	Español

Inglés	Ilustración/dibujo	Español

Inglés	Ilustración/dibujo	Español

Inglés	Ilustración/dibujo	Español

Inglés	Ilustración/dibujo	Español

Reproducible A.7:
Planning Grid for Using Latino Parents to Augment Lessons

Content Area	Grade-Level Standard Addressed This Week	Ideas
Reading		
Writing		
Math		
Social Studies		
Science		

Reproducible A.8a: Invitation to Parent–Teacher Conference

Dear Parent:

The purpose of this note is to invite you to come to our classroom. I would like to see you to discuss how your son/daughter, ____________________________, is doing in class. I would like to share with you the many learning opportunities we have in our classroom, as well as discuss a recurring issue that I hope you can help me with.

Please call me at ____________________________ or stop by our classroom so we can talk about days/times that are convenient for you for our conference.

Thank you,

Your child's teacher

Reproducible A.8b:
Invitación a una Conferencia de Padres y Maestros

Estimado(a) padre/madre:

El propósito de esta nota es invitario(a) a que venga a nuestro salón. Me gustaría verlo(a) para discutir cómo va su hijo(a), ____________________, en la escuela. Hemos tenido muchas oportunidades de aprendizaje en nuestro salón que me gustaría compartir con usted. Asimismo, quiero que hablemos de un tema recurrente con el que espero que me pueda ayudar.

Por favor llámeme al teléfono ____________________ o pase por mi salón para hablar de qué día y a qué hora le gustaría tener nuestra conferencia.

Muchas gracias,

El/la maestro(a) de su hijo(a)

Reproducible A.9a:
Letter to Parents About the Multiple Intelligences

Dear Parent:

One of the most respected professors of education and leading psychologists of our time is Dr. Howard Gardner, who teaches at the prestigious Harvard University. Dr. Gardner has written more than 20 books and several hundred articles focused largely on intelligence. Some of his most famous books are titled *Extraordinary Minds*, *The Development and Education of the Mind*, and *Multiple Intelligences: New Horizons*. Dr. Gardner has changed the way educators think about intelligence. He defines intelligence as

> "The capacity to solve problems or to fashion products that are valued in one or more cultural settings."

In short, this means that intelligence can be measured in varied ways rather than by one IQ score, which implies that children can be smart in many different ways.

As of today, Dr. Gardner has identified eight separate kinds of intelligence. These are the following:

1. Verbal/linguistic	Children who learn best through language and who prefer to communicate with others through listening, speaking, reading, and writing. These children like words and learning them; can make rhymes easily; like to tell stories; can learn a different language quickly.
2. Logical/mathematical	Children who learn best by solving problems and reasoning things out. These children like working with numbers; solving problems; to reason; to analyze systems and their components.
3. Visual/spatial	Children who learn best when representing information visually. These children like making images; working or looking at pictures, graphs, charts, etc.; to web their ideas.
4. Bodily/kinesthetic	Children who learn best through action and hands-on activities. These children like to use all or parts of their body. They like dance, moving around, making crafts, and athletics.
5. Musical	Children whose best learning is linked to their sense of rhythm and music. These children like sound—to listen to it, make it, and manipulate it.

Reproducible A.9a:
Letter to Parents About the Multiple Intelligences (*continued*)

6. Interpersonal — Children who learn best when working with others. These children are considered "people smart" because they can recognize the intentions and feelings of others. They are sensitive to what others are going through.

7. Intrapersonal — Children who learn best through reflection, sharing, and working alone. These children are "self smart" because they can reflect on their feelings, strengths, and weaknesses and make meaning in their lives.

8. Naturalistic — Children who like to figure out how things work in the natural surroundings. These children like to grow plants, care for animals and the environment, and may be interested in the weather.

Children can be strong in more than one intelligence; in fact, Dr. Gardner believes that each child has a blend of the intelligences. I am sending you this letter so that you will think about how your child might be intelligent and how you can move toward enhancing his or her multiple intelligences. The following table presents some ways that you can help your child.

If your child is...	Think about having your child...
Verbal/linguistic	• Debate a simple topic (e.g., "Why should I buy you sugary cereals?"). • Make a speech (e.g., "Tell us five good reasons why you can watch an extra hour of TV"). • Keep a daily journal (buy one or make one with your child and have him or her write freely on specific topics e.g., "I want you to write about what you would do if you won a million dollars"). • Write letters (e.g., to a loved one, the school principal, a neighbor, or a community leader). • Tell stories (e.g., "I'm going to tell you a story, and I want you to end it").
Logical/mathematical	• Investigate a problem (e.g., "Why does the sink leak?" or "What can we do so that no one trips on that step?"). • Create a survey (e.g., "Ask your friends if you should cut, curl, or dye your hair"). • Make a puzzle (e.g., reassemble a cut-up magazine photo or a photograph). • Find patterns (e.g., "Design a floor pattern for the kitchen"). • Record information (e.g., list what is needed from the grocery store).
Visual/spatial	• Draw (e.g., "Draw me three pictures of the sea for the living room"). • Paint. • Illustrate (e.g., "Let's make a comic book about...."). • Make a poster (e.g., "Make a sign with reasons to turn off the lights"). • Take photographs (e.g., "I want you to take pictures of everyone in the family doing something funny").

Reproducible A.9a:
Letter to Parents About the Multiple Intelligences (*continued*)

If your child is...	Think about having your child...
Bodily/kinesthetic	• Perform creative movements (e.g., play charades, trying to guess particular animals). • Act in a play (e.g., "I want you to act out the story your teacher read to you today"). • Role-play (e.g., "Pretend that you are me and I am you"). • Construct models (e.g., make a gingerbread house, a birdhouse, a doll house out of cardboard). • Conduct experiments.
Musical	• Compose lyrics (e.g., "Let's write some music for a poem we write"). • Write a song (e.g., "How could we change the song or add to it?"). • Make a musical instrument out of household products. • Play a musical instrument.
Interpersonal	• Participate in group activities. • Organize a party (e.g., "How should we celebrate Christmas this year?"). • Volunteer.
Intrapersonal	• Keep a personal diary. • Set personal goals.
Naturalistic	• Make observations about the surroundings (e.g., "Let's go to the park and collect as many leaves as possible"). • Identify and solve environmental problems (e.g., "What could we do so that people won't litter anymore?"). • Make predictions or comparisons. • Classify objects.

Whenever you interact with your child, please use some of these ideas or come up with some of your own. If you have any questions, need more suggestions, or want my help to identify your child's multiple intelligences, please contact me at ______________________________.

Sincerely,

Your child's teacher

Reproducible A.9b:
Carta a los Padres Acerca de las Inteligencias Múltiples

Estimado(a) padre/madre:

Uno de los profesores de educación y psicólogos más respetados de nuestros tiempos es el Dr. Howard Gardner, quien enseña en la prestigiosa Universidad de Harvard. El Dr. Gardner ha escrito 22 libros y varios cientos de artículos que se centran mayormente en la inteligencia. Algunos de sus libros más famosos tienen títulos como *Mentes Extraordinarias, El Desarrollo y Educación de la Mente,* e *Inteligencias Múltiples: Nuevos Horizontes.* El Dr. Gardner ha cambiado la manera en la que los educadores piensan acerca de la inteligencia. El Dr. Gardner define la inteligencia como

> "la capacidad de resolver problemas o desarrollar productos con valor en más de un ambiente cultural."

En resumen, esto significa que la inteligencia se puede medir de varias formas, no solamente con un resultado de coeficiente intelectual. En otras palabras, esto implica que los niños pueden ser inteligentes en más de una manera.

Hasta ahora, el Dr. Gardner ha identificado ocho tipos diferentes de inteligencia. Estos incluyen:

1. Verbal/lingüística	Los niños(as) que aprenden mejor a través del lenguaje y que prefieren comunicarse con otros escuchando, hablando, leyendo y escribiendo. A estos niños(as): les gusta aprender palabras; pueden hacer rimas fácilmente; les gusta contar historias; pueden aprender un lenguaje diferente rápidamente.
2. Lógica/matemática	Los niños(as) que aprenden mejor resolviendo problemas y razonando las cosas. A estos niños(as) les gusta: trabajar con números; resolver problemas; razonar; analizar sistemas y sus componentes.
3. Visual/espacial	Los niños(as) que aprenden mejor cuando representan la información visualmente. A estos niños(as) les gusta: hacer imágenes; trabajar con o ver dibujos; gráficas, etc.; hacer esquemas con sus ideas.
4. Corporal/kinestética	Los niños(as) que aprenden mejor a través de la acción y actividades que pueden hacer con sus manos. A estos niños(as) les gusta usar todas las partes de su cuerpo. A ellos(as) les gusta bailar, moverse, hacer artesanías y atletismo.
5. Musical	Los niños(as) que aprenden mejor cuando su aprendizaje se relaciona con su sentido del ritmo y la música. A estos niños(as) les gusta el sonido: escucharlo, hacerlo y manipularlo.

Reproducible A.9b:
Carta a los Padres Acerca de las Inteligencias Múltiples (*continued*)

6. Interpersonal — Los niños(as) que aprenden mejor cuando trabajan con otros. A estos niños se les considera "inteligentes con la gente" porque pueden reconocer las intenciones y sentimientos de otros. Son perceptivos(as) de lo que les pasa a los demás.

7. Intrapersonal — Los niños(as) que aprenden mejor cuando pueden reflexionar, compartir, y trabajar solos(as). Estos niños(as) son "inteligentes de sí mismos(as)" porque pueden reflexionar acerca de sus sentimientos, sus destrezas, debilidades y encontrar el significado en sus vidas.

8. Naturalista — Los niños(as) que aprenden mejor cuando tratan de adivinar cómo funcionan las cosas en sus alrededores. A estos niños(as) les gusta sembrar plantas, cuidar a los animales, el medio ambiente; también les puede llamar la atención el clima.

Los niños(as) pueden tener destrezas en más de una inteligencia. De hecho, el Dr. Gardner cree que cada niño(a) tiene una combinación de inteligencias. Le mando esta carta para que usted piense qué tipo de inteligencia tiene su hijo(a) y cómo puede ayudarle a sacar provecho de sus inteligencias múltiples. Estas son algunas maneras en las que usted puede ayudar a su hijo(a):

Si su hijo(a) es...	Piense en hacer que su hijo(a)...
Verbal/lingüístico	• Debata un tema simple; por ejemplo, "¿Por qué crees que debo comprar cereal azucarado?" • Haga un discurso; por ejemplo, "Dame cinco buenas razones para ver la televisión una hora más." • Mantenga un diario (puede comprar o hacer uno con su hijo/a) donde puede escribir libremente o acerca de temas específicos; por ejemplo, "Quiero que escribas qué harías si te ganaras un millón de dólares." • Escriba cartas; por ejemplo, puede escribir una carta a un ser querido, al director de la escuela, a un vecino o a un líder comunitario. • Cuente historias; por ejemplo, "Voy a contarte una historia y quiero que tú pienses en cuál sería el final."
Lógica/matemática	• Investigue un problema; por ejemplo, "¿Por qué chorrea el lavabo?" o "¿Qué podemos hacer para que no se tropiece nadie con ese escalón?" • Haga una encuesta; por ejemplo, "pregúntales a tus amigos si piensan que te deberías cortar, rizar o pintar el pelo." • Haga un rompecabezas; por ejemplo, arme una fotografia cortada de una revista. • Encuentre patrones; por ejemplo, "Diseña un patrón de piso para la cocina." • Documente información; por ejemplo, una lista de lo que se necesita de la tienda.

Reproducible A.9b:
Carta a los Padres Acerca de las Inteligencias Múltiples (*continued*)

Si su hijo(a) es...	Piense en hacer que su hijo(a)...
Visual/espacial	• Dibuje; por ejemplo, "Hazme tres dibujos del mar para poner en la sala." • Pinte. • Ilustre; por ejemplo, "Vamos a hacer una tira cómica de. . . ." • Haga un póster; por ejemplo, "Haz un anuncio con las razones por las cuales debes apagar la luz." • Tome fotografías; por ejemplo, "Quiero que tomes fotos de tu familia haciendo algo cómico o chistoso."
Corporal/kinestética	• Haga movimientos creativos; por ejemplo, participe en juegos tratando de adivinar animales, palabras, etc. • Actúe en una obra; por ejemplo, "Quiero que actúes la historia que leyó tu maestra en la escuela." • Actúe; por ejemplo, "Haz de cuenta que tú eres yo y yo soy tú. . . ." • Construya modelos; por ejemplo, una casa con galletas, una casa para pájaros o una casa de cartón para muñecas. • Haga experimentos.
Musical	• Componga la letra de una canción; por ejemplo, "Vamos a escribir música para un poema nuestro." • Escriba una canción; por ejemplo, "¿Cómo podemos cambiar la canción o agregarle algo?" • Haga un instrumento musical con productos que tiene en casa. • Toque un instrumento musical.
Interpersonal	• Participe en actividades de grupo. • Organice una fiesta; por ejemplo, "¿Cómo vamos a celebrar la Navidad este año?" • Haga trabajo de voluntario.
Intrapersonal	• Mantenga un diario personal. • Se ponga metas a sí mismo(a).
Naturalista	• Haga observaciones de sus alrededores; por ejemplo, "Vamos al parque a juntar cuantas hojas sea posible." • Identifique y resuelva problemas ambientales; por ejemplo, "¿Qué podemos hacer para que la gente ya no tire basura?" • Haga predicciones o comparaciones. • Clasifique objetos.

Cada vez que interactúe con su hijo(a), por favor use algunas de estas ideas u otras que se le ocurran. Si tiene cualquier pregunta, necesita más sugerencias o quiere mi ayuda para identificar las inteligencias múltiples de su hijo(a), por favor comuníquese conmigo al ______________________________.

Sinceramente,

El/la maestro(a) de su hijo(a)

Reproducible A.10a: Homework Is Wonderful

Dear Parents:

I trust that all is well with you and your family. Today, I spoke with the students about their responsibility for doing homework. I mentioned that homework is beneficial for—

Teachers, because homework . . .

- Allows for another person to reteach the student a concept or skill in a different, and sometimes better, way.
- Helps students master grade-level objectives.
- Can involve fun, meaningful, and challenging assignments.
- Helps us evaluate the student's progress and tailor our lessons accordingly.
- Helps us celebrate with you when the child is successful.

Parents, because homework . . .

- Allows you to spend time with your child.
- Helps you to understand how well your child masters grade-level concepts and skills, giving you firsthand knowledge of your child's abilities.
- Allows you the opportunity to teach your child using your background knowledge to complement the grade-level content.
- Helps you understand the teacher's expectations.

Children, because homework . . .

- Helps them refine their skills and strengthen their understanding of grade-level content.
- Enriches their abilities and general knowledge base.
- Helps them learn the importance of time and task management.

If homework is a challenge for you and your child, or if you would like to discuss any aspect of homework with me, please feel free to contact me at your earliest convenience.

Sincerely,

Your child's teacher

Reproducible A10.b: La Tarea Es Maravillosa

Estimado(a) padre/madre:

Espero todo se encuentre bien con usted y su familia. El día de hoy, hablé con los estudiantes acerca de la responsabilidad que implica el hacer tarea. Les mencioné que la tarea es un beneficio para—

Maestros/maestras, porque la tarea . . .

- Permite que otra persona le vuelva a enseñar al estudiante un concepto o destreza de una manera diferente y, algunas veces, de una mejor manera.
- Ayuda a los estudiantes a lograr los objetivos de su nivel.
- Puede incluir actividades que representan retos divertidos y con sentido.
- Nos ayuda a evaluar el progreso del estudiante y a modificar nuestras lecciones de acuerdo a este progreso.
- Nos ayuda a celebrar con usted cuando el niño(a) tiene éxito.

El padre/la madre, porque la tarea . . .

- Le permite pasar tiempo con su hijo(a).
- Le ayuda a entender qué tan bien el niño(a) entiende los conceptos y destrezas a su nivel y a tener un mejor conocimiento de las destrezas de su hijo(a).
- Le da la oportunidad de enseñar a su hijo(a) usando el conocimiento que usted tiene para complementar el contenido del nivel o año escolar del niño(a).
- Le ayuda a entender las expectativas del maestro(a).

Niños/niñas, porque la tarea . . .

- Les ayuda a refinar sus destrezas y entender mejor el contenido de su nivel o año escolar.
- Enriquece sus habilidades y base su conocimiento general.
- Les ayuda a aprender la importancia de manejar su tiempo y tareas.

Si la tarea es un reto para usted y su hijo(a), o si le gustaría discutir cualquier aspecto de la tarea conmigo, por favor siéntase con la confianza de ponerse en contacto conmigo cuando le sea más conveniente.

Sinceramente,

El/la maetro(a) de su hijo(a)

Reproducible A.11a:
A Note to the Teacher: The Assignment Was Too Difficult

Child's name: ______________________________ Date: ______________

Assignment: ____

Dear Teacher:

My child had a difficult time completing the homework mentioned above. In particular,

_____ The concepts were too difficult.

____

____

_____ The instructions were not clear.

____

____

_____ The assignment was overwhelming.

____

____

_____ The assignment took too long to complete.

____

____

_____ The reading was too long for my child.

____

____

_____ The reading was too complicated and difficult to comprehend.

____

____

Here are some ideas that would help me and my child complete homework:

____

____

Sincerely,

Parent

Phone Number:

Best Times to Call:

Reproducible A.11b:
Una Nota para el Maestroa: La Tarea Estaba Muy Difícil

Nombre del niño(a): ______________________________ Fecha: ______________

Tarea: ____

Estimado(a) Maestro(a):

A mi hijo(a) se le hizo difícil completar la tarea que se describe arriba. En particular,

______ Los conceptos eran muy difíciles.

____

____

______ Las instrucciones no estaban claras.

____

____

______ Era mucha tarea.

____

____

______ Tomó mucho tiempo completar la tarea.

____

____

______ La lectura era muy larga para mi hijo(a).

____

____

______ La lectura era muy complicada y difícil de entender.

____

____

Estas son algunas ideas que nos ayudarían a mi hijo(a) y a mí a completar la tarea:

____

____

Sinceramente,

Padre/madre

Número de teléfono:

Mejores horas para llamar:

Reproducible A.12a: Homework Sheet

Name: ______________________________ Week of: ______________

Date	Subject Area	Page No.	Special Note	Completed	Grade

Important Announcements:

Parent Signature ______________________________ Date ______________

Reproducible A.12b: Hoja de Tarea

Nombre: ______________________ Semana de: ______________

Fecha	Área/Materia	Número de Página	Nota Especial	Terminado	Calificación

Anuncios Importantes:

Firma del padre/madre ______________________ Fecha ______________

Reproducible A.13a: Homework Policy

Dear parent:

The district's homework policy can be found in the Parent Student Handbook; however, today I discussed my homework policy with the students. Please take the time to review the policy described below with your children so that they fully understand my expectations.

- I assign homework on ________________ (Monday, Tuesday, Wednesday, Thursday)
  Every day of the week
  Monday through Thursday

- I assign homework that reinforces grade-level goals, has been covered in class, and can be successfully completed in reasonable time.

- I assign homework that is challenging and meets students' needs and abilities.

- I tend to give ____________________ (reading, math, spelling, social studies, science) tests and quizzes on ____________________ (Monday, Tuesday, Wednesday, Thursday, Friday).

- I assign about ________________ (30 minutes, one hour, 1½ hours, 2 hours) worth of homework every night.

- Occasionally, your child will have a project to do, which can take several evenings to complete, but additional information about it will follow in separate letters.

- Please make sure that your child reads at least ________________ minutes every evening.

- The children will use an agenda book that the school provides to organize their homework information. Before leaving for home, the children will neatly write their assignments and related directions in their agendas. Please be sure to ask your child for the agenda and review it together to ensure that your child has followed the homework directions precisely. Also, be sure that you ask if your child has his or her homework when leaving for school the next day. I will gather the homework the next morning, review it with the students, and return it graded as soon as I can. As often as possible, encourage your child to do the homework, and give praise when your child is successful.

OR

- I will provide a homework sheet and folder for your child. Before leaving for home, the students will neatly write their assignments and respective directions on the homework sheet. Please be sure to ask your child for the homework sheet and folder. In one pocket you will find the homework sheet, which details the instructions for homework; in the other pocket you can expect to find the graded

Reproducible A.13a: Homework Policy (*continued*)

homework, which you can use to measure your child's achievement. Please review the homework sheet with your child to ensure that the homework directions have been followed precisely. Be sure to ask if your child has his or her homework when leaving home for school the next day. I will gather the homework the next morning, review it with the students, and return it graded as soon as I can. The grade will be noted on the homework sheet, which I ask that you sign at the end of the week. As often as possible, encourage your child to do the homework, and give praise when your child is successful.

- I often use homework as the basis for your child's grades, which are reflected on the report card.

- I use homework as my own measure of your child's achievement and tailor my instruction accordingly.

- If homework is not complete and the student is excused, he or she is expected to turn it in late (and may receive a lower grade). Please send a note with your child or have your child explain the circumstances that warrant the acceptance of a late assignment. Students not excused will ________________ (stay after school to complete it and turn it in late for a lower grade; will not have the opportunity to turn it in late and will receive a zero; will lose a classroom privilege).

Please let me know if your child consistently has difficulty with the homework, and always feel free to send me comments and questions.

Thank you,

Your child's teacher

Reproducible A.13b: Política de Tarea

Estimado(a) padre/madre:

La política de tarea del distrito escolar puede encontrarse en el Manual para Padres de los Estudiantes; sin embargo, hoy discutí mi política de tarea con los estudiantes. Por favor haga el tiempo para discutir con su hijo(a) la política que se describe a continuación para que entiendan cuáles son mis expectativas.

- Asigno tarea el ________________ (lunes, martes, miércoles, jueves)
  Cada día de la semana
  De lunes a jueves

- Asigno tarea que refuerza las metas del nivel o año escolar de su niño(a), hemos cubierto en clase y pueden ser terminadas en un tiempo razonable.

- Asigno tarea que representa un reto para los estudiantes y que va de acuerdo con sus necesidades y habilidades.

- Administro exámenes de ________________ (lectura, matemáticas, deletreo, estudios sociales, ciencia) el ________________ (lunes, martes, miércoles, jueves, viernes).

- Asigno aproximadamente ________________ (30 minutos, 1 hora, 1 hora y media, 2 horas) de tarea cada noche.

- De vez en cuando, su hijo(a) tendrá que hacer un proyecto, que puede tomar varias noches para completar. Luego se mandarán cartas para darle más información de estos proyectos.

- Por favor asegúrese de que su hijo(a) lea al menos ________________ minutos cada noche.

- Los niños(as) usarán una agenda para organizar la información de su tarea. Antes de irse a casa, escribirán en sus agendas las asignaturas e instrucciones para completar la tarea. Por favor asegúrese de preguntarle a su hijo(a) por la agenda y de repasarla con él/ella para asegurarse de que siga las instrucciones para completar la tarea. También asegúrese de preguntarle al niño(a) si él/ella tiene su tarea antes de salir de la casa a la escuela al día siguiente. Yo recogeré la tarea a la mañana siguiente, la repasaré con los estudiantes y la regresaré calificada en cuanto pueda. Tan seguido como sea posible, anime a su hijo(a) a hacer su tarea y elógielo cuando tenga éxito.

O

- Le daré una hoja o folder de tarea a su niño(a). Antes de irse a casa, los estudiantes escribirán los deberes, tarea o asignatura y las instrucciones para completarlos. Por favor asegúrese de preguntarle por la hoja o folder a su hijo(a). De un lado del folder, encontrará la hoja de tarea con instrucciones

Reproducible A.13b: Política de Tarea (*continued*)

detalladas para hacer la tarea. En el otro lado estará la tarea calificada para que vea los logros de su niña(a). Por favor repase la hoja de tarea con él/ell para asegurarse de que hayan seguido las instrucciones. También pregunte a su hijo(a) si tiene su tarea con él/ella antes de salir de casa para ir a la escuela al día siguiente. Yo recogeré la tarea a la mañana siguiente, la repasaré con los estudiantes, y la regresaré tan pronto como pueda. La calificación estará escrita en la hoja de tarea, la cual le pido que firme al final de la semana. Tan seguido como le sea posible, anime a su hijo(a) a hacer su tarea y elógielo cuando tenga éxito.

- Algunas veces uso la tarea como base para las calificaciones de su niño(a), que se reflejan en la tarjeta de calificaciones.

- Uso la tarea para darme cuenta de los logros de su hijo(a) y para modificar mi enseñanza o instrucción de acuerdo a ello.

- Si la tarea no está completa y el estudiante tiene una excusa, se espera que él/ella entregue la tarea tarde (y puede recibir una calificación más baja). Por favor mande una nota con su hijo(a) o pídale que explique por qué tuvo que entregar la tarea tarde. Los estudiantes que no tengan excusa tendrán que ________________ (quedarse después de la escuela para completar la tarea y entregarla tarde para recibir una calificación más baja; perder la oportunidad de entregarla tarde y recibir un cero; perder un privilegio de clase).

Por favor hágame saber si su hijo(a) a tiene problemas persistentes con la tarea y siéntase siempre con la confianza de mandarme sus comentarios y preguntas.

Gracias,

El/la maestro(a) de su hijo(a)

Reproducible A.14a: Supplies for the Homework/Study Area

Dear Parents:

Children have an easier time completing their homework when the resources they need are found in one location. Stock the homework/study area with as many of these supplies as possible:

- Paper
- Pens
- Pencils
- Erasers
- Scissors
- Markers
- Crayons (or colored pencils)
- Scrap paper
- Calculator
- Glue
- Tape
- Dictionary
- Thesaurus

If you have any other supply ideas to share with other parents, please let me know.

Sincerely,

Your child's teacher

Reproducible A.14b: Materiales para el Área de Tarea/Estudio

Estimado(a) padre/madre:

Los niños pueden completar mejor su tarea cuando tienen los recursos necesarios para hacerla en un solo sitio. Usted puede crear un área de tarea o estudio con los materiales que le sean posibles, tales como:

- Papel
- Plumas
- Lápices
- Borradores
- Tijeras
- Marcadores o plumones
- Crayolas, colores de cera, o lápices de color
- Pedazos de papel para escribir
- Calculadora
- Goma, pegamento
- Cinta adhesiva
- Diccionario
- Libro de sinónimos/antónimos

Si tiene alguna otra idea de qué materiales incluir en esta área para compartir con otros padres, por favor hágame saber.

Sinceramente,

El/la maestro(a) de su hijo(a)

Reproducible A.15a: Homework Chart

Feel free to use this chart—or create a similar one of your own—to remind you and your child to complete homework when it is assigned. Have your child write the assignment in the appropriate box, check off the smaller box when it is complete, and later note the grade. Then, together you can decide on the reward to enjoy when the homework is finished.

Day	Reading	Writing	Social Studies	Science	Math	Other	Reward
Monday	☐	☐	☐	☐	☐	☐	
Tuesday	☐	☐	☐	☐	☐	☐	
Wednesday	☐	☐	☐	☐	☐	☐	
Thursday	☐	☐	☐	☐	☐	☐	
Friday	☐	☐	☐	☐	☐	☐	

Reproducible A.15b: Gráfica de Tarea

Puede usar esta gráfica—o algo parecido que usted haga—para recordarles a su hijo(a) y a usted que hay que completar la tarea. Pídale a su niño(a) que escriba sus asignaturas o tarea en el espacio respectivo, marque con una X cuando la complete y después escriba la calificación que reciba. Cuando la tarea esté terminada, su hijo(a) y usted pueden decidir juntos qué premio o recompensa se le dará al niño(a) por haber cumplido con sus deberes.

Día	Lectura	Escritura	Estudios Sociales	Ciencia	Matemáticas	Otro	Recompensa
Lunes	☐	☐	☐	☐	☐	☐	
Martes	☐	☐	☐	☐	☐	☐	
Miércoles	☐	☐	☐	☐	☐	☐	
Jueves	☐	☐	☐	☐	☐	☐	
Viernes	☐	☐	☐	☐	☐	☐	

Reproducible A.16a: A Note About Homework

Dear Parents:

As we start a new school year, please consider the following ideas, which may help you help your child successfully complete homework.

First, make it a routine to ask your children for the homework that is assigned. Rather than ask, "Do you have homework tonight?" instead ask, "What homework do you have tonight?" And follow with, "How does it relate to what you did in class today?" Also, establish a homework time that is consistent every school night. Homework time can occur immediately when the children get home from school or some time after they have rested, relaxed, or played outside. Or it can occur well into the evening before bedtime. In other words, establish the time when it is most convenient for you and your family.

Second, during homework time, enforce rules that create a good climate for studying. For instance—

- No TV, video games, or music playing
- No phone calls
- No computer or Internet usage, unless it is for homework
- No friends visiting

During homework time, ask that everyone be quiet. Family members without homework obligations can pursue other constructive activities (like reading, drawing, or a home-based science experiment).

Third, create a reasonable place in your home to do homework. You and your child can locate an appropriate area. It should be comfortable, well lit, and free from as many distractions as possible (away from the phone, TV, and so forth). Kitchen and dining room tables are often ideal because they allow children to spread out their books and materials. The homework area should become known as *the* study area to go to when homework needs to be done. Your child can even decorate the area with signs that say "Do Not Disturb," "Work in Progress," or "Achiever at Work."

Next, because children have an easier time completing their homework when the resources they need are in one place, stock the homework/study area with as many of these supplies as possible:

Paper	Pens	Pencils	Erasers	Scissors	Crayons/colored pencils
Markers	Scrap paper	Calculator	Glue	Tape	Dictionary
Thesaurus					

Reproducible A.16a: A Note About Homework (*continued*)

Feel free to use this chart—or create a similar one of your own—to remind you and your child to complete homework when it is assigned. Have your child write the assignment in the respective box, and after you have reviewed it for neatness and accuracy, check off the smaller box when it is complete and later note the grade. I can provide you a copy of this chart each week if you would like.

Day	Reading	Writing	Social Studies	Science	Math	Other	Reward
Monday	☐	☐	☐	☐	☐	☐	
Tuesday	☐	☐	☐	☐	☐	☐	
Wednesday	☐	☐	☐	☐	☐	☐	
Thursday	☐	☐	☐	☐	☐	☐	
Friday	☐	☐	☐	☐	☐	☐	

Reproducible A.16a: A Note About Homework (*continued*)

Last, remember to offer praise when your child is successful with homework. Perhaps you and your child can make a list of reasonable rewards (such as spending some special time together or playing outside) to enjoy when the homework is finished. I will be sure to send notes home when I am proud of your child's accomplishments.

Please let me know if you have any other ideas that I can share with other parents. If you have any questions, comments, or concerns, please feel free to write your reply below. And always let me know what I can do to help you fulfill your child's needs.

Sincerely,

Your child's teacher

Parent's Reply:

Reproducible A.16b: Unas Palabras Acerca de la Tarea

Estimado(a) padre/madre:

Al comenzar un nuevo año escolar, por favor considere las siguientes ideas, que pueden ayudarle a ayudar a que su hijo complete su hijo(a) con éxito.

Primero, siga la rutina de preguntarles a sus hijos(as) qué tienen de tarea. En lugar de preguntar, "¿Tienes tarea?," pregunte "¿Qué tienes de tarea?" y continúe con, "¿Cómo se relaciona con lo que aprendiste en clase hoy?" También establezca una hora para hacer la tarea que sea la misma cada noche. La tarea se puede hacer inmediatamente cuando llegan los niños de la escuela, o después de que descansen un poco o jueguen afuera. También se puede hacer por la tarde o antes de ir a la cama. En otras palabras, establezca una hora que sea conveniente para usted y su familia.

Segundo, durante la hora de la tarea, establezca reglas para crear un ambiente de estudio. Por ejemplo—

- Sin televisión, juegos de video, o música
- Sin llamadas telefónicas
- Sin uso de computadora o Internet, al menos que sea para para la tarea
- Sin amigos

Durante la hora de la tarea, procure que haya silencio. Los miembros de la familia que no tienen tarea pueden hacer otras actividades constructivas (como leer, dibujar, hacer un experimento de ciencia con materiales disponibles en casa, etc.).

Tercero, haga un espacio en su casa que esté disponible para hacer tarea. Su hijo(a) y usted pueden encontrar un área en la casa donde se pueda completar la tarea. Debe ser un lugar con buena luz y tan libre de distracciones como sea posible (lejos del teléfono, la televisión, etc.). Las mesas de la cocina o el comedor pueden ser un lugar ideal porque tienen espacio suficiente para los niños. A esta área de tarea se le debe conocer como el área de estudio donde debe hacerse la tarea. Su niño(a) puede hasta decorar el área con anuncios que digan "No Molestar" o "Trabajo en Progreso."

Después, porque es más fácil que los niños hagan su tarea cuando tienen los recursos necesarios, puede tener algunos de estos materiales en el área de estudio:

Papel	Plumas	Lápices	Borradores	Tijeras	Colores
Marcadores	Calculadora	Goma	Cinta adhesiva	Diccionario	

Reproducible A.16b: Unas Palabras Acerca de la Tarea (*continued*)

Por último, puede usar esta gráfica—o crear una parecida—para recordarles su hijo(a) y a usted que debe completar la tarea. Pídale niño(a) que escriba la tarea en el espacio respectivo y después de revisarla, marque con una X cuando la tarea esté completa. Si gusta puedo darle una copia de esta gráfica cada semana.

Día	Lectura	Escritura	Estudios Sociales	Ciencia	Matemáticas	Otro	Recompensa
Lunes	☐	☐	☐	☐	☐	☐	
Martes	☐	☐	☐	☐	☐	☐	
Miércoles	☐	☐	☐	☐	☐	☐	
Jueves	☐	☐	☐	☐	☐	☐	
Viernes	☐	☐	☐	☐	☐	☐	

Reproducible A.16b: Unas Palabras Acerca de la Tarea (*continued*)

Por último, recuerde darle ánimo a su hijo(a) cuando él/ella tenga éxito con su tarea. Quizá él/ella y usted pueden hacer una lista de recompensas/premios razonables (pasar tiempo juntos, jugar fuera, etc.) para disfrutar cuando la tarea esté terminada. Yo mandaré notas a casa para informarle acerca de los logros de su hijo(a).

Por favor hágame saber si tiene alguna otra idea que yo pueda compartir con otros padres. Si tiene cualquier pregunta, comentario o queja, por favor siéntase con la libertad de escribir su respuesta abajo. Hágame saber lo que puedo hacer para ayudarle con las necesidades de su hijo(a).

Sinceramente,

El/la maestro(a) de su hijo(a)

Respuesta del Padre/de la madre:

Reproducible A.17a: Homework Certificates

Kudos to You!

____

Did an awesome job on this homework assignment!

____

Your Teacher

____

Date

Way to Go!

____

What a fantastic job on your homework!

____

Your Teacher

____

Date

I'm Beaming with Pride!

____

Excellent homework!

____

Your Teacher

____

Date

Reproducible A.17b: Certificados de Tarea

¡Felicidades!

____

¡Un trabajo excelente en tu tarea!

____

Tu maestro(a)

____

Fecha

¡Bien hecho!

____

¡Un trabajo fantástico en tu tarea!

____

Tu maestro(a)

____

Fecha

Me Siento Orgulloso(a) de

____

¡Excelente tarea!

____

Tu maestro(a)

____

Fecha

Reproducible A.18a: Homework Notes

A Homework Request

Dear Parents:

I have grown concerned recently because your child is not benefiting from the homework that I have been assigning. I have noticed that—

________ The homework is incomplete.

________ The homework is sloppy.

________ The homework is not turned in.

________ The homework is late.

________ The homework seems carelessly completed.

________ Other: ____
____
____
____
____
____.

________ I have noticed that ____
____
____
____
____
____
____.

Will you please talk to your child about the importance of doing the best possible job when completing homework? Also, let me know if there is anything I can do to help you help your child complete the homework successfully.

Sincerely,

Your child's teacher ____

Date ____________________

Reproducible A.18a: Homework Notes (*continued*)

A Homework Boost

Dear Parents:

I have noticed that your child has some difficulty with—

____

____

____

____

____

____.

To help facilitate your child's understanding, I am sending home this assignment:

________ See the attached.

________ Other: ____

____

____

____

____

____

____

____

____

____.

Please take a moment to review the assignment with your child, reteach the skill or concept as best you can, and guide your child through the work without giving the answers.

If you have any questions, comments, or concerns, please feel free to let me know.

Sincerely,

Your child's teacher ______________________________________

Date ____________________

Reproducible A.18b: Una Nota de Tarea

Un Pedido de Tarea

Estimado(a) padre/madre:

Me preocupa que su hijo(a) no se beneficie con la tarea que se le ha asignado. He notado que—

________ La tarea está incompleta.

________ La tarea está descuidada.

________ La tarea no está siendo entregada.

________ La tarea se entrega tarde.

________ La tarea se completó sin cuidado.

________ Otro: ____

____

____

____

____

____.

________ Me he dado cuenta de que:______________________________

____

____

____

____

____.

Por favor hable con su hijo(a) acerca de la importancia de aplicarse al hacer su tarea. Además avíseme si hay algo que yo pueda hacer para ayudarlo a que usted ayude a su niño(a) a completar su tarea con éxito.

Sinceramente,

El/la maestro(a) de su hijo(a) ____________________________

Fecha ________________

Reproducible A.18b: Una Nota de Tarea (*continued*)

Animo para la Tarea

Estimado(a) padre/madre:

Me he dado cuenta de que su hijo(a) tiene dificultad con—

____

____

____

____

____

____.

Para ayudarlo(a) a entender mejor, mando el siguiente trabajo a casa:

________ Vea el papel adjunto.

________ Otro: ____

____

____

____

____

____

____

____

____

____.

Por favor tome un momento para repasar la tarea con su hijo(a), enseñarle el concepto o destreza lo mejor que usted pueda y guiar al niño(a) en el trabajo sin darle las respuestas.

Si tiene cualquier pregunta, comentario, o queja, por favor hágame saber.

Sinceramente,

El/la maestro(a) de su hijo(a) ____________________________________

Fecha ____________________

Reproducible A.19a: Letter to Parent About Neighborhood Walk

Dear Parents:

In our next unit of study, we will be learning about the neighborhood where we live. We will be engaged in many learning activities, one of which includes taking a class walk around our school neighborhood on ______________________________ (date).

I am asking your permission for your child, ______________________________, to accompany us on this walk. Let me know if you would like to join us. We would appreciate your company on our learning walk.

Your signature below indicates your permission for your child to participate.

Thank you,

Your child's teacher

____ ____________________

Parent's signature Date

____ ____________________

Parent's name Date

Reproducible A.19b:
Carta a los Padres Acerca de un Paseo por la Comunidad

Estimado(a) padre/madre:

En nuestra siguiente unidad de estudio, vamos a aprender acerca del vecindario/barrio/colonia en donde vivimos. Participaremos en muchas actividades de aprendizaje. Una de ellas incluye una caminata/paseo de la clase alrededor del vecindario/barrio/colonia en ________________________ (fecha).

Pedimos su permiso para que su hijo/a, ________________________, nos pueda acompañar en esta caminata/paseo. Si le es posible, nos gustaría que usted también nos acompañara en nuestra caminata/paseo de aprendizaje.

Su firma abajo indica su permiso para que su hijo/a participe.

Muchas gracias,

El/la maestro(a) de su hijo/a

________________________________ ________________

Firma del padre/de la madre Fecha

________________________________ ________________

Nombre del padre/de la madre Fecha

Reproducible A.20a:
Structuring a Plan to Increase Latino Parental Involvement

1. Assign a team member as the recorder to complete the form and track progress over time.
2. Select a task to focus on (e.g., strengthening the PTA). The reproducible can be photocopied for each designated task the team chooses at any given time.
3. The tasks of the subgroup are arbitrary and are at the discretion of the team (e.g., students may not have any role in strengthening the PTA).
4. Using the "Level of Change" scale, decide whether the task is initiating, intermediate, advanced, or ongoing, depending on the productivity of the team. The level of change can remain stable or advance to the next level. The evaluation of the level of change is based on the team's observations.

	Parents	Students	PTA	Teacher Leaders	Grade-Level Chairs	Administrators	Counselors	Other Staff Members
Task(s):								
How this sub-group within the organization can contribute								
Level of expected change Date:								

Reproducible A.20a:
Structuring a Plan to Increase Latino Parental Involvement (*continued*)

	Parents	Students	PTA	Teacher Leaders	Grade-Level Chairs	Administrators	Counselors	Other Staff Members
Individuals assigned								
Documentation needed from each subgroup								
Observations								
Date: Assess progress								

Levels of Change:
- 0 = Ongoing
- 1 = Initiating
- 2 = Intermediate
- 3 = Advanced Progress

Reproducible A.20b:
Structuring a Plan to Increase Latino Parental Involvement (Example)

	Parents	Students	PTA	Teacher Leaders	Grade-Level Chairs	Administrators	Counselors	Other Staff Members
Task(s): *Strengthen parental involvement in PTA*	*X*		*X*	*X*		*X*		*Instructional coordinator: Mrs. Correa*
How this subgroup within the organization can contribute	*Bring one parent to meeting*		*Provide light refreshments and sponsor student performance*	*Organize student performance*		*Welcome parents*		*Briefly discuss three tips for standardized testing preparation*
Level of expected change Date: *Aug. 28*	*1*		*Ongoing*	*1*		*Ongoing*		*Ongoing*
Individuals assigned			*PTA leadership team*	*All*		*Mr. Mendez*		*Mrs. Correa*

Reproducible A.20b:

Structuring a Plan to Increase Latino Parental Involvement (Example) (*continued*)

	Parents	Students	PTA	Teacher Leaders	Grade-Level Chairs	Administrators	Counselors	Other Staff Members
Documentation needed from each subgroup			*Agenda*	*Program of student performance*				*Handouts*
Observations	*10 parents came*		*Shows have been amazing*	*Shows have been amazing*		*Good reports*		*Parents like the three tips*
Date: *Dec. 7* Assess progress	*2*		*Ongoing*	*2*		*Ongoing*		*Ongoing*

Levels of Change:

- 0 = Ongoing
- 1 = Initiating
- 2 = Intermediate
- 3 = Advanced progress

Reproducible A.21:
Fall/Winter/Spring Reports on Latino Parental Involvement

Latino Parent Meetings Fall 20____ Report

[Parent name and contact information are on file and available from sign-in sheets submitted.]

Latino Parent Meetings	September	October	November	December
Grade Level: PreK–Kindergarten 1st 2nd 3rd 4th 5th				
PTA/PTO				
Muffins for Mom				
Donuts for Dads				
Literacy Night				
Math Night				
Technology Night				
Science Fair				
Annual Carnival				
Annual BBQ				
Adult ESL Classes				

Reproducible A.21:
Fall/Winter/Spring Reports on Latino Parental Involvement (*continued*)

Latino Parent Meetings Winter/Spring 20____ Report

[Parent name and contact information are on file and available from sign-in sheets submitted.]

Latino Parent Meetings	January	February	March	April
Grade Level: PreK–Kindergarten 1st 2nd 3rd 4th 5th				
PTA/PTO				
Muffins for Mom				
Donuts for Dads				
Literacy Night				
Math Night				
Technology Night				
Science Fair				
Annual Carnival				
Annual BBQ				
Adult ESL Classes				

Reproducible A.21:
Fall/Winter/Spring Reports on Latino Parental Involvement (*continued*)

Latino Parent Meetings Spring 20____ Report

[Parent name and contact information are on file and available from sign-in sheets submitted.]

Latino Parent Meetings	May	June	Comments	Notes
Grade Level: PreK–Kindergarten 1st 2nd 3rd 4th 5th				
PTA/PTO				
Muffins for Mom				
Donuts for Dads				
Literacy Night				
Math Night				
Technology Night				
Science Fair				
Annual Carnival				
Annual BBQ				
Adult ESL Classes				

APPENDIX B

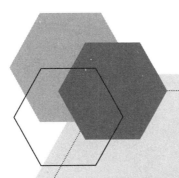

Websites Devoted to Latino Culture

Hispanic Society of America Museum and Library
http://www.hispanicsociety.org

The website for this museum in New York City displays an array of photos that showcase the Spanish, Portuguese, and Latin American artifacts in its collection. A number of links lead to background information on pieces related to archaeology, decorative arts, paintings, sculptures, and textiles.

National Hispanic Cultural Center
http://www.nationalhispaniccenter.org

Since opening in 2000, the center, which is in Albuquerque, New Mexico, has held many art exhibitions and programs in the visual, performing, and literary arts. The website features links to the images of the permanent collection coupled with background information about the artists and their respective works. Future plans include providing online access to their publications, digital gallery, and support materials for educators.

Latin American Network Information Center
http://lanic.utexas.edu

A center for resources devoted to matters associated with Latin America, this website provides links to other websites, blogs, articles, and other sources, with browsing organized by country or subject (economy, education, humanities, and so on). Databases afford access to full-text articles and other print resources.

Benson Latin American Collection
http://www.lib.utexas.edu/benson/index.html

This website provides background information on the holdings specific to Latino American Studies and Mexican American and Latino Studies at the University of Texas. Site visitors can access online publications and images from the exhibits.

Hispanic Online
http://www.hispaniconline.com

Hispanic magazine operates this website, which highlights some of the magazine's most current feature articles, as well as the latest news (from other sources) central to the lives of Hispanics.

Gale Cengage Learning: Hispanic Heritage
http://www.gale.cengage.com/free_resources/chh

This wonderful website for teachers features ideas for classroom activities associated with various Hispanic customs and celebrations, comprehensive biographies of more than 50 important Hispanics, a historical perspective on Hispanic musical genres, an online quiz on Hispanics, and a time line (beginning with 1492) of events important to Hispanics.

Diego Rivera Virtual Web Museum
http://www.diegorivera.com/index.php

This website provides extensive information about Rivera's life and work, along with photos from the art gallery, well-known murals, and video footage.

Handbook of Latin American Studies
http://lcweb2.loc.gov/hlas

This Library of Congress website is a bibliography of selected scholarship (in social science and humanities) related to Latin America. Each year more than 5,000 pieces of work are selected for inclusion in the site. A link allows site visitors to search the database.

Scholastic: Celebrate Hispanic Heritage Month
http://teacher.scholastic.com/activities/hispanic

Teachers can use this wonderful website to learn more about the Hispanic culture as well as to teach about it to students. Links provide access to information on key moments in Hispanic history, biographical information on noteworthy Hispanics, and an interactive game students can use to learn some Spanish words. A Research Starter button leads to a wide range of ideas (and background information) for lesson plans and classroom activities.

National Registry of Historic Places
http://www.nps.gov/history/nr/feature/hispanic

The registry celebrates National Hispanic Heritage Month (September 15--October 15) by listing places that underscore the contributions of Hispanic culture and achievement in American history. Website visitors can access background information on the locations, which all have architectural and artistic significance.

APPENDIX C

Books on Latino Culture

Customs, Celebrations, and Other Cultural Elements

- *Everything You Need to Know About Latino History*, by Himilce Novas (2008). Presented in a question-and-answer format, this excellent reference guide covers many issues of interest to Latinos in the United States, including popular culture as exemplified by TV shows, such as *Ugly Betty*, and Latino baseball players.
- *The Complete Idiot's Guide to Latino History and Culture*, by Danilo H. Figueredo (2002). This quick reference guide to Latino culture describes demographic trends specific to Latinos and discusses 400 years of Latinos' contributions to the United States.

Social and Political Topics

- *Hispanics in the United States: An Agenda for the Twenty-first Century*, edited by Pastora San Juan Cafferty and David W. Engstrom (2002). Covering a wide range of topics that affect Latinos, the authors provide demographic information in their discussions of immigration, religious practices, the labor market, health, and welfare trends. Two chapters relate specifically to language and education.
- *Latinos and the Nation's Future*, edited by Henry G. Cisneros (2009). Scholars share their ideas about how they believe Hispanics are shaping the future of the United States, covering topics such as demographics, political contributions, mobility rates, and issues related to health, housing, and other social trends.

Literature

- *The Latino Reader: An American Literary Tradition from 1542 to the Present*, edited by Harold Augenbraum and Margarite Fernandez (1997). This is a wonderful anthology of literature by Latino writers. Scholars have assembled historical and autobiographical works, and essays by Cuban, Mexican American, and Puerto Rican writers, among others.
- *The Prentice Hall Anthology of Latino Literature*, edited by Eduardo Del Rio (2001). The essays in this anthology are written by Latinos with lived experiences in the United States. The authors write primarily in English, and their literary work reflects their heritage within the American culture. The book features short stories, poems, and plays by well-known writers such as Sandra Cisneros, Luis Valdez, Cristina Garcia, and others.

Educating Latino Youth

- *Teaching Hispanic Children*, by Toni Griego Jones and Mary Lou Fuller (2003). This book has a number of aspects that make it worth reading, particularly the first few chapters that challenge teachers' beliefs about Hispanic youth and the unprecedented trends they are setting. A chapter is devoted to the history of Mexico and other Hispanic countries. Additional chapters focus on language issues and strategies for the classroom.
- *Latino Education: An Agenda for Community Action Research,* edited by Pedro Pedraza and Melissa Rivera (2005). This book combines theoretical discussion of the instruction of Latino youth and advocacy strategies for their success. More than 20 Latino scholars share their views on topics such as the history of Latino/a education, standards reform and its effect on Latinos, social action for Latino students, and the future of Latino education.

APPENDIX D

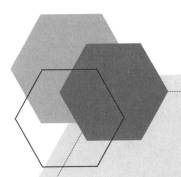

Children's Books for Latino Students

Abuela, by Arthur Dorros (1991). A child and her grandmother rise into the air to go on an imaginary trip over Manhattan. As they fly away and look at all the sights below them, Spanish words and phrases are integrated in the English text.

Abuela's Weave/El Tapiz de Abuela, by Omar S. Castañeda (1993). After weaving colored tapestries in their Guatemalan village, Esperanza and her *abuela* (grandmother) take the bus to sell their work at an outdoor market. When they sell all their goods, both women return home proudly sharing a bus seat, as well as the joy of their hard work and the special bond between them.

Abuelita's Secret Matzahs/Las Matzás Secretas de Abuelita, by Sandy Eisenberg Sasso (2005). Jacobo learns from his *abuelita* (grandmother) that their family celebrates *Semana Santa* (Holy Week) differently from others. During Jacobo's visit, *abuelita* shares the family's secret and tells Jacobo about Jewish traditions.

Carolina's Gift: A Story of Peru, by Katacha Díaz (2002). Carolina gets her grandmother a walking stick as a birthday present so that they can go to the market together. As Carolina goes through the market stalls looking for the perfect gift, Spanish words for the items she finds there are introduced.

Chato's Kitchen/Chato y Su Cena, by Gary Soto and Susan Guevara (1995). This is the story of two cats, Chato and Novio Boy, that live in East L.A. and have a group of mice as neighbors.

A Day's Work, by Eve Bunting (1994). Francisco is a young boy who acts as interpreter between his grandfather and the man who hires him to do work, assuming that *abuelo* (grandfather) is a gardener. Francisco does not tell the man that his grandfather is, in fact, a carpenter. After wrongly completing the job, *abuelo* finds out Francisco lied to the man and refuses to get paid, teaching his grandson a lesson in integrity.

Día de Mercado, by Lois Ehlert (2002). This book takes the reader on a journey around the world to visit different market stands and all the articles found in them.

Esperanza Rising/Esperanza Renace, by Pam Munoz Ryan (2000). This is the story of Esperanza, a Mexican girl who immigrates to the United States and has to adapt to a new culture and different social class in her new country.

Family Pictures/Cuadros de Familia, by Carmen Lomas Garza (1990). This book presents a series of paintings depicting the author's childhood memories of growing up in South Texas.

The Girl from Chimel, by Rigoberta Menchú (2000). Rigoberta Menchú, 1992 Nobel Peace Prize winner, shares a memoir of her childhood growing up in the indigenous village of Chimel, Guatemala.

Gracias the Thanksgiving Turkey/Gracias el Pavo de Thanksgiving, by Joy Cowley (1998). Miguel hopes that his *papá* (dad) will make it home in time for Thanksgiving but worries that his pet turkey, Gracias, will become the dinner. After he gets lost and is recovered, Gracias gets blessed by a priest in New York City and cannot be eaten anymore. Throughout the book, the reader learns some Spanish words used in the story, and at the end, Miguel and Gracias enjoy a great Thanksgiving with their family.

Grandfather and the Three Bears/Abuelo y los Tres Osos, by Jerry Tello (1997). This is the Hispanic version of "Goldilocks and the Three Bears." It can be read in English or Spanish by turning the book upside-down.

I Hate English, by Ellen Levine (1989). This story is told through the eyes of a recently arrived Asian immigrant who struggles to make sense of the English language and to communicate in it. With her teacher's help, the main character goes through the different stages of learning the language of a new country.

I Love Saturdays y Domingos, by Alma Flor Ada (2002). This is the story of a bilingual girl who spends alternate weekends at her English-speaking paternal grandparents' house or that of her Mexican American *abuelitos*, who speak to her in Spanish. As she recognizes the similarities in both households, the main character learns to see cultural and linguistic differences as strengths rather than hardships.

In My Family/En Mi Familia, by Carmen Lomas Garza (2005). This book presents a series of paintings depicting everyday events, as well as special moments in the author's Mexican American family.

La Mariposa, by Francisco Jiménez (1998). Francisco is confused and does poorly in school because he does not understand the language (English) his teachers and classmates speak. His communication difficulties cause him to withdraw, and rather than trying to speak, he prefers to watch and draw a caterpillar in a jar on the science shelf. By the end of the year, he is like the butterfly that has emerged from a cocoon.

My Diary from Here to There/Mi Diario de Aquí Hasta Allá, by Amada Irma Pérez (2002). This is the story of Amada's family move from Juárez, Mexico, to Los Angeles, California, and her worries about moving away from everything that is familiar to her.

My Name Is Jorge: On Both Sides of the River, by Jane Medina (1999). This book of poems presents the migrant experience from the perspective of children and the challenges encountered in adjusting to a new language and culture.

The Night of the Posadas/La Noche de las Posadas, by Tomie DePaola (1999). This is the story of Las Posadas, an old Hispanic custom celebrated in December. The background and history of this tradition are provided, as well as a glossary with English translations of Spanish words used in the text.

The Night the Moon Fell/La Noche Que Se Cayó la Luna, by Pat Mora (2000). This is a retelling of the Mayan myth of how the Milky Way was created when *luna* (the moon) broke into pieces upon falling from the sky.

Pablo and Pimienta/Pablo y Pimienta, by Ruth M. Covault (1998). This bilingual picture book documents the experiences of Pablo, a migrant child. When he falls off the back of his dad's truck, Pablo befriends a coyote and names it Pimienta. Together, they find their way back to the watermelon fields where Pablo's family works on the U.S. border.

Papa Tells Chita a Story, by Elizabeth Fitzgerald Howard (1995). Chita's father shares stories from when he was in the army during the Spanish-American War and had to deliver messages across the island of Cuba, overcoming many dangers.

Pepita Talks Twice/Pepita Habla Dos Veces, by Ofelia Dumas Lachtman (1995). Pepita becomes frustrated when she has to speak both Spanish and English. When she decides to speak English only, she realizes she is missing out on some of her family's and friends' traditions (e.g., singing in Spanish). She later learns about the importance of being bilingual when Spanish helps her prevent her pet from having an accident.

Pepita Thinks Pink/Pepita y el Color Rosa, by Ofelia Dumas Lachtman (1995). Although Pepita does not like pink, she learns to accept differences in taste when she finds out that pink is her neighbor friend's favorite color.

The Piñata Maker/El Piñatero, by George Ancona (1994). This book documents a day in the life of a piñata maker. The steps to create piñatas in different shapes are discussed, as well as the artistic abilities of the people who make them. Through its bilingual text, the book provides an introduction to an important Hispanic custom.

The Rainbow Tulip/El Tulipán Arco Iris, by Pat Mora (1994). This book describes the home and early school experiences of a young girl, Estelita, as she continues to develop her identity as Mexican American.

Saturday Sancocho/El Sancocho del Sábado, by Leyla Torres (1995). A girl and her grandmother go through the *mercado* (market) looking for the ingredients they need to make *sancocho*, a stew made of meat and vegetables.

Smoky Night/Noche de Humo, by Eve Bunting (1995). In this picture book, two neighboring families do not talk or help each other until the building where they live catches on fire. At that point, all of the neighbors learn about the importance of bridging differences to prevent urban violence.

The Story of Colors/La Historia de los Colores, by Subcomandante Marcos (1999). This is an indigenous story that explains how the gods created the colors. As the colors combine to make more colors, the gods chose the macaw's feathers as a place to keep them safe.

Thomas and the Library Lady/Tomás y la Señora de la Biblioteca, by Pat Mora (1997). This book tells the story of one summer in the life of Tomás Rivera, chancellor of the University of California at Riverside, who grew up in a migrant family. While his family works in the fields, Tomás meets a librarian in Iowa who fosters his love for books and reading.

Too Many Tamales/¡Qué Montón de Tamales! by Gary Soto and Ed Martínez (1993). While Maria is learning how to make *tamales* with her relatives, she loses a ring in the dough. She worries that someone will eat the ring but later finds out one of her relatives found the ring before cooking the *tamales.* The importance of always telling the truth is highlighted in this book.

There's a Frog in My Throat! 440 Animal Sayings a Little Bird Told Me, by Loreen Leedy and Pat Street (2003). This book presents numerous English sayings with definitions and illustrations, making it a great language tool/resource for students who may have difficulties with understanding the meaning of everyday expressions.

The Upside Down Boy/El Niño de Cabeza, by Juan Felipe Herrera (2000). This is the story of Juanito, a Hispanic boy who feels his world has been turned upside down when he has to adjust to being a student in an American school. With his family's and teacher's support, Juanito adjusts to the new culture very well.

Who Let the Cat Out of the Bag? by 4th-grade students of Newcastle Avenue Elementary in Reseda, California (2002). This book introduces idioms to children and provides illustrations of how non-native English speakers may interpret the meaning of each saying.

APPENDIX E

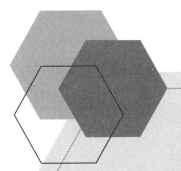

Examples of Homework Policies

Northeast Independent School District, San Antonio, Texas

Homework is an integral part of a child's learning process. It may be assigned as reinforcement of materials introduced in class or of material not completed in class. If the teacher gives an assignment, the student is expected to complete and return it to class on time and in a neat manner. Parents can help to encourage proper completion of assignments by providing a specific time and place for study. Lesson assignments may be requested through the office, generally after three consecutive days of absence. Teachers need adequate time to gather and prepare assignments. Please contact the school to find out the place and time of day to collect your child's homework.

Source: NEISD. (2010). *Student–parent handbook.* Retrieved August 1, 2010, from http://www.neisd.net/pupil/studenthb.html

San Francisco Unified School District, San Francisco, California

Homework is scheduled as part of the instructional program at each grade level. The time required to complete such teacher-assigned work should not exceed 20 minutes per day in grades K–3 and 30 minutes per day at grades 4–5. Specific information regarding homework shall be planned at each site involving staff and parents/guardians/caregivers. Parents/guardians/caregivers will be informed of this policy at the start of each school year.

Source: SFUSD. (2010). *Student and parent/guardian handbook.* Retrieved August 1, 2010, from http://portal.sfusd.edu/data/pupil/Student_Handbook_English.pdf

Hillsborough County Public Schools, Tampa, Florida

A student has the right to:

- meaningful and relevant homework activity that reinforces school learning;
- homework that matches their individual abilities and interests to ensure the facilitation of independent, successful completion;
- homework that includes varied activities which reinforce the basic skills or extend and enrich concepts learned;
- homework that does not introduce new concepts;
- assignments that are made according to individual student needs and abilities;
- regular feedback to include parents regarding assignment. Parents should be notified when a student routinely does not complete homework.

Homework assignments:

- Should not be punitive in nature;
- Should not require students to have specific resources such as Internet access;
- Should be coordinated among team members so as not to exceed the recommended amount of time devoted to homework;
- Should not exceed a total of 15 to 20 minutes per night for kindergarten, a total of 30 minutes per night for students in Grades 1, 2, 3, and 45 minutes per night in Grades 4 and 5. It is recommended that homework not be assigned on Fridays with special consideration given around testing and holidays;
- Appropriate completion of homework assignments will be reflected in the Expected Behaviors section of the K–5 Report Card.

Source: Hillsborough County Public Schools. (2010). *Know the rules… know your rights: Student handbook.* Retrieved August 1, 2010, from http://www.sdhc.k12.fl.us/AdminDiv/Documents/StudentHandbook/0910StudentHandbook.pdf

Steinway Intermediate School 141Q,
NYC Department of Education, New York, New York

Homework is a three-way partnership:

- The teacher will provide a quality assignment each night.
- The student will complete all assignments neatly and submit the homework on a daily basis to each respective teacher.
- The parent/guardian will monitor and encourage completion of all home assignments/projects.
- Call the school immediately if your child frequently tells you there is no homework (there is homework every night).
- Write a note if your child is struggling with an assignment or you have an emergency that prevents homework from getting done.

Agenda Book

Each student was issued an agenda book on the first day of school.

A student's responsibility:

- To make sure that all assignments are written in your agenda before leaving at the end of the day
- To write all directions carefully to make sure that assignments are completed correctly

- To use the agenda while doing homework
- To check off each item as it is completed
- To add upcoming events, due dates and assignments, test dates, and other personal dates to your monthly calendar

A parent's responsibility:

- To make sure that all assignments are clearly written each night
- To check that all parts of the assignments are completed
- To look for, and respond to, teachers comments
- To feel free to add comments or questions to the teacher

Source: I.S. 141 The Steinway. (2010). *Parent handbook*. Retrieved August 2, 2010, from http://schools.nyc.gov/SchoolPortals/30/Q141/TopLinks/Parent+Handbook.htm

References & Resources

American Civil Liberties Union (ACLU). (2007, March 6). ACLU challenges prison-like conditions at Hutto Detention Center. Available: http://www.aclu.org/immigrants-rights-racial-justice/aclu-challenges-prison-conditions-hutto-detention-center)

American Federation of Teachers. (2004). Closing the Achievement gap: Focus on Latino students. *AFT Policy Brief, 17*, 1–7.

Banks, J. A. (1993). Approaches to multicultural curriculum reform. In J. A. Banks & C. A. M. Banks (Eds.), *Multicultural education*. Boston: Allyn & Bacon.

Bennett, S., & Kalish, N. (2006). *The case against homework: How homework is hurting our children and what we can do about it.* New York: Crown.

Bialystok, E. (2007). Acquisition of literacy in bilingual children: A framework for research. *Language Learning, 57*(1), 45–77.

Brisk, M. E., & Harrington, M. M. (2007). *Literacy and bilingualism: A handbook for all teachers.* Mahwah, NJ: Lawrence Erlbaum.

Carr, R. (1980). *Puerto Rico: A colonial experiment.* New York: New York University Prcss.

Carrera, J. W. (1992). *Immigrant students: Their legal right of access to public schools. A guide for advocates and educators.* Boston: National Coalition of Advocates for Students. (ERIC Document Reproduction Service No. ED 381588)

Catts, H. W., & Kamhi, A. G. (Eds.). (1999). *Language and reading disabilities.* Boston: Allyn & Bacon.

Children's Defense Fund. (2007). *America's cradle to prison report: A report to the Children's Defense Fund.* Retrieved January 29, 2011, from http://nicic.gov/Library/022726

Chong, N., & Baez, F. (2005). *Latino culture.* Yarmouth, ME: Intercultural Press.

Communities in Schools. (2009). *Helping kids stay in school and prepare for life.* Retrieved July 21, 2009, from http://www.cisnet.org/default.asp

Cooper, H. (1989). Synthesis of research on homework. *Educational Leadership, 47*(3), 85–91.

Cooper, H. (2007). *The battle over homework* (3rd ed.). Thousand Oaks, CA: Corwin Press.

Cooper, H., Robinson, J., & Patall, E. (2006). Does homework improve academic achievement? A synthesis of research, 1987–2003. *Review of Educational Research, 76*(1), 1–62.

Core Knowledge Foundation. (1999). *Core knowledge sequence: Content guidelines for grades K–8.* Charlottesville, VA: Author.

Cummins, J. (2000). *Language, power and pedagogy: Bilingual children in the crossfire.* Clevedon, UK: Multilingual Matters.

Davis, A. (2004). *Ways to use weblogs in education.* Retrieved July 15, 2009, from http://anne2.teachesme.com/2004/10/05/

Diaz-Rico, L. T. (2004). *Teaching English learners: Strategies and methods.* Boston: Pearson.

Dominguez, F. (1957). *The missions of New Mexico, 1776.* Albuquerque, NM: University of New Mexico Press.

Duke, N., & Purcell-Gates, V. (2003). Genres at home and at school: Bridging the known to the new. *The Reading Teacher, 57*(1), 30–37.

Durgunoğlu, A. Y., & Verhoeven, L. (Eds.). (1998). Acquiring literacy in English and Spanish in the United States. *Literacy development in a multilingual context: Cross-cultural perspectives* (pp. 135–145). Mahwah, NJ: Lawrence Erlbaum.

Foster, J., Aguero, R., Harrison, K., & Delgado, R. (1999). *Action research grant summary.* Center for Teaching Excellence. Portales, NM: Eastern New Mexico University.

Fredricks, J., & Eccles, J. (2006). Extracurricular involvement and adolescent adjustment: Impact of duration, number of activities, and breadth of participation. *Applied Developmental Science, 10,* 132–146.

Gann, L., & Duignan, R. (1986). *The Hispanics in the United States: A history.* Boulder, CO: Westview.

García, O. (2009). *Bilingual education in the 21st century: A global perspective.* Malden, MA: Wiley-Blackwell.

Gardner, H. (1993). *Frames of mind: The theory of multiple intelligences.* New York: Basic Books.

Gay, G. (2000). *Culturally responsive teaching: Theory, research, and practice.* New York: Teachers College Press.

Gee, J. P. (1996). *Social linguistics and literacies: Ideology in discourses.* London: Taylor & Francis.

Genesee, F., Lindholm-Leary, K., Saunders, B., & Christian, D. (2006). *Educating English language learners: A synthesis of research evidence.* New York: Cambridge University Press.

González, N., Moll, L. C., Floyd, T. M., Rivera, A., et al. (1995). Funds of knowledge for teaching in Latino households. *Urban Education, 29*(4), 443–447.

Gutiérrez-Clellen, V. F., Calderón, J., & Weismer, E. (2004). Verbal working memory in bilingual children. *Journal of Speech, Language, and Hearing Research, 47*(4), 863–876.

Heath, S. B. (1983). *Ways with words: Language, life, and work in communities and classrooms.* New York: Cambridge University Press.

Kemmis, S., & McTaggart, R. (2000). Participatory action research. In N. K. Denzin & Y. S. Lincoln (Eds.), *Handbook of qualitative research.* Thousand Oaks, CA: Sage.

Kindler, A. (2002). *Survey of the states' limited English proficient students and available educational programs and services: 2000–2001 summary report.* Retrieved February 19, 2006, from http://www.ncela.gwu.edu/states/index.htm

Kirkland, L. D., & Patterson, J. (2005). Developing oral language in primary classrooms. *Early Childhood Education Journal, 32*(6): 391–395.

Kohn, A. (2006). *The homework myth: Why our kids get too much of a bad thing.* Cambridge, MA: Da Capo Press.

Kozulin, A. (Ed.) (2000). *Thought and language: Lev Vygotsky.* Cambridge, MA: MIT Press.

Kralovec, E., & Buell, J. (2000). *The end of homework: How homework disrupts families, overburdens children, and limits learning.* Boston: Beacon.

Ladson-Billings, B. (1992). Reading between the lines and beyond the pages: A culturally relevant approach to literacy teaching. *Theory into Practice, 31*(4), 312–320.

Lindholm-Leary, K., & Borsato, G. (2006). Academic achievement. In F. Genesee, K. Lindholm-Leary, W. M. Saunders, & D. Christian (Eds.), *Educating English language learners: A synthesis of research evidence* (pp. 176–222). New York: Cambridge University Press.

Margolis, H. (2005). Resolving struggling learner's homework difficulties: Working with elementary school learners and parents. *Preventing School Failure, 50*(1), 5–12.

Martinez, O. (2001). *Mexican-origin people in the United States: A topical history.* Tucson, AZ: University of Arizona Press.

McIntyre, E., Rosebery, A., & Gonzalez, N. (2001). *Classroom diversity: Connecting curriculum to students' lives.* Portsmouth, NH: Heinemann.

McLaren, P. (2009). Critical pedagogy: A look at the major concepts. In A. Darder, M. P. Baltodano, & R. D. Torres (Eds.), *The critical pedagogy reader* (pp. 61–83). New York: Routledge.

Moll, L. C., Amanti, C., Neff, D., & Gonzalez, N. (1992). Funds of knowledge for teaching: Using a qualitative approach to connect homes and classrooms. *Theory into Practice, 31*(2), 132–141.

Moran, R. (2009, April). *It's not just about equality: English language learners and the freedom to learn.* Paper presented at the meeting of the American Educational Research Association, San Diego, CA.

National Campaign to Stop Violence. (2010). *Help stop school & youth violence!* Retrieved July 27, 2010, from http://www.dtwt.org

National Center for Education Statistics. (2006). *Public elementary and secondary students, staff, schools, and school districts: School year 2003–2004.* Retrieved June 3, 2010, from http://nces.ed.gov/pubsearch/pubsinfo.asp?pubid=2006307

National Center for Education Statistics. (2008). *The condition of education 2008.* (NCES Publication No. 2008-031). Washington, DC: U.S. Department of Education.

Nieto, S., Bode, P., & Bode, P. (2007). *Affirming diversity: The sociopolitical context of multicultural education* (5th ed.). New York: Pearson/Allyn and Bacon.

Noddings, N. (2002). *Educating moral people: A caring alternative to character education.* New York: Teachers College Press.

Ogbu, J. U. (1998). Voluntary and involuntary minorities: A cultural-ecological theory of school performance with some implication for education. *Anthropology and Education Quarterly, 29*(2), 155–188.

Olivos. (2006). *The power of parents: A critical perspective of bicultural parents in public schools.* New York: Peter Lang Publishing, Inc.

Pellegrini & Galda. (1993). Ten years after: A reexamination of symbolic play and literacy research. *Reading Research Quarterly, 28*(2), 162–175.

Pérez, B. (2000). *Creating a sociocultural context for school literacy.* New York: Pearson.

Pérez, B. (2004). *Sociocultural contexts of language and literacy.* Mahwah, NJ: Lawrence Erlbaum.

Pérez, B., & Torres-Guzmán, M. E. (2002). *Learning in two worlds: An integrated Spanish/English biliteracy approach.* Boston: Allyn & Bacon.

Pew Hispanic Center. (2006a). *From 200 million to 300 million: The numbers behind population growth.* Retrieved July 15, 2010, from http://pewhispanic.org/publications/?year=2006

Pew Hispanic Center. (2006b). *A statistical portrait of Hispanics at mid-decade.* Retrieved July 15, 2010, from http://pewhispanic.org/publications/?year=2006

Pinker, S. (1995). Language acquisition. In L. R. Gleitman & M. Liberman (Eds.), *Language: An invitation to cognitive science* (2nd ed., pp. 135–182). Cambridge, MA: MIT Press.

Quiocho, M. L., & Daoud, A. M. (2006). Dispelling myths about Latino parent participation in schools. *Educational Forum, 6*(3), 255–267.

Ramírez, A. Y. (2003). Dismay and disappointment: Parental involvement of Latino immigrant parents. *The Urban Review, 35*(2), 93–110.

Ritchie, D. A. (2003). *Doing history: A practical guide.* New York: Oxford University Press.

Romaine, S. (2001). *Bilingualism* (2nd ed.). Malden, MA: Blackwell Publishers.

Schmidt, P. (2005). *Academe's Hispanic future.* Retrieved July 22, 2010, from http://csma.aas.org/spectrum_files/spectrum_Jun05.pdf

Scribner, J. D., Young, M. D., & Pedroza, A. (1999). Building collaborative relationships with parents. In P. Reyes, J. D. Scribner, & A. Paredes Scribner (Eds.), *Lessons from high performing Hispanic schools: Creating learning communities* (pp. 36–60). Williston, VT: Teachers College Press.

Shonkoff, J. P., & Phillips, D. A. (Eds.) (2000). *From neurons to neighborhoods: The science of early child development.* Washington, DC: National Academy Press.

Smith, M. K. (2008). *Howard Gardner and multiple intelligences: The encyclopedia of informal education.* Retrieved July 3, 2010, from http://www.infed.org/thinkers/Gardner.htm

Sosa, A. S. (1997). Involving Hispanic parents in educational activities through collaborative relationships. *Bilingual Research Journal, 21*(2&3), 1–8.

Texas Education Agency (2009). *Framework for the language proficiency assessment committee process.* Retrieved July 17, 2009, from http://ritter.tea.state.tx.us/curriculum/biling/lpacmanual/LPAC.ppt

Thomas, W., & Collier, V. P. (2002). *A national study of school effectiveness for language minority students' long term academic achievement: Final report.* Retrieved July 9, 2010, from http://crede.berkeley.edu/research/llaa/1.1_final.html

Thompson, M. M., & Winn Tutwiler, S. J. (2001). Coaching the after-school instructional staff. *Educational Leadership, 58*(7), 56–58.

Tomás Rivera Policy Institute. (2004). *The new Latino South and the challenge to public education: Strategies for educators and policymakers in emerging immigrant communities.* Retrieved July 20, 2010, from http://www.eric.ed.gov/PDFS/ED502060.pdf

Trueba, H. (1999). *Latinos unidos: From cultural diversity to the politics of solidarity.* New York: Rowman & Littlefield.

U.S. Census Bureau (2000). *Language use and English-speaking ability: 2000.* Washington, DC: Author. Retrieved July 29, 2009, from http://www.census.gov/prod/2003pubs/c2kbr-29.pdf

Vygotsky, L. S. (1986). *Thought and language.* Cambridge, MA: MIT.

Wade, R. C. (1997). *Community service-learning: A guide to including service in the public school curriculum.* Albany, NY: SUNY Press.

Zentella, A. C. (1997). *Growing up bilingual.* Malden, MA: Blackwell.

Index

The letter *f* following a page number denotes a figure.

About the Authors

David Campos began his education career more than 15 years ago when he started teaching 2nd grade. He later entered graduate school, taught ESL, and worked in corporate training and development. In 1996, he earned his Ph.D. at the University of Texas at Austin, specializing in learning disabilities and behavior disorders. His first job in academia was at Roosevelt University in Chicago, where he was an Assistant Professor in the College of Education. There he served as Director of the Metropolitan Institute for Teaching and Learning and was an Acting Assistant Dean of Academic Affairs. After earning rank and tenure he accepted an Associate Professor of Education position at the University of the Incarnate Word in San Antonio, Texas.

He has written three books grounded in youth sexuality: *Sex, Youth, and Sex Education*; *Diverse Sexuality in Schools*; and *Understanding Gay and Lesbian Youth*. Additionally, his most recent book is *Expanding Waistlines: An Educator's Guide to Childhood Obesity*. He has also coauthored a resource text and evaluation instrument for teachers of English language learners titled *Practical Ideas That Really Work for English Language Learners*. His peer-reviewed articles focus on constructivist teaching and authentic assessment by way of African American visionaries. Dr. Campos traveled to China in 2004 on a Fulbright grant. Dr. Campos can be reached at 210-283-5029 or campos@uiwtx.edu.

Rocio Delgado holds a Ph.D. from the University of Texas at Austin and is an Assistant Professor and Special Education Program Director at Trinity University in San Antonio, Texas. Her research interests include the education of culturally and linguistically diverse students with or without disabilities and collaboration among school professionals and students' families. In addition to teaching graduate and undergraduate education courses, Dr. Delgado supervises teaching interns in general, bilingual/ ESL, and special education settings. As a former community educator, parent advisor, early intervention program assistant, and bilingual teacher in Mexico, Dr. Delgado has also worked with families of recent immigrants and in developing and translating programs for Spanish-speaking parents.

Dr. Delgado's previous publications include contributions to education textbooks (*Planning as a Team, Learning Together*; *Language Disorder or Language Difference: Sol's Story*; *Creating/Building Communities in Adult Education*) and articles in peer-reviewed journals ("The Instructional Dynamics of a Bilingual Teacher: One Teacher's Beliefs About English Language Learners"; "Poco a Poquito Se Van Apagando: Teachers' Experiences in Educating English Language Learners with Disabilities"; "A Teacher's Journey in Working with English Language Learners with/without Disabilities"). Dr. Delgado can be reached at 210-999-7672 or rocio.delgado@trinity.edu.

Mary Esther Soto Huerta received her Ph.D. from the University of Texas at San Antonio. Currently she is an Assistant Professor of Culture, Literacy, and Language at Texas State University–San Marcos, where she teaches courses in bilingual education, ESL, and reading in the College of Education. Her research focuses on issues concerning biliteracy, language and literacy development in bilingual settings, bilingualism, issues of equity in education for language-minority students, and bilingual teacher education.

Dr. Soto Huerta was a bilingual education teacher and as a teacher specialist supervised bilingual education teachers and wrote curriculum for two school districts. Dr. Soto Huerta has presented her research nationally. Some of her published articles include "Using Cultural Tools to Develop Scientific Literacy of Mexican American Preschoolers"; "Fourth Grade Biliteracy: Searching for Instructional Footholds"; "Biliteracy as a Unitary Process"; "Finding Voice, Defining Self: An Interview with Yuyi Morales" (on bilingual writing); and "Credentialing Foreign-Trained Teachers." Dr. Soto Huerta can be reached at 512-245-3099 or mh75@txstate.edu.

Related ASCD Resources: English Language Learners

At the time of publication, the following ASCD resources were available (ASCD stock numbers appear in parentheses). For up-to-date information about ASCD resources, go to www.ascd.org.

Print Products

Classroom Instruction That Works with English Language Learners by Kathleen Flynn and Jane Hill (#106009)

Getting Started with English Language Learners: How Educators Can Meet the Challenge by Judie Haynes (#106048)

Meeting the Needs of Second Language Learners: An Educator's Guide by Judith Lessow-Hurley (#102043)

The Language-Rich Classroom: A Research-Based Framework for Teaching English Language Learners by Persida Himmele and William Himmele (#108037)

Videos and DVDs

Maximizing Learning for English Language Learners (three 35-minute videotapes with facilitator's guide) (#403326)

Raising the Literacy Achievement of English Language Learners (one DVD with facilitator's guide) (#606122)

A Visit to a Classroom of English Language Learners (one 45-minute videotape with viewer's guide) (#404447)

THE WHOLE CHILD The Whole Child Initiative helps schools and communities create learning environments that allow students to be healthy, safe, engaged, supported, and challenged. To learn more about other books and resources that relate to the whole child, visit www.wholechildeducation.org.

For more information: send e-mail to member@ascd.org; call 1-800-933-2723 or 703-578-9600, press 2; send a fax to 703-575-5400; or write to Information Services, ASCD, 1703 N. Beauregard St., Alexandria, VA 22311-1714 USA.